COMMEMORATIVE MEDALS
OF THE QUEEN'S REIGN
IN CANADA, 1952-2012

COMMEMORATIVE MEDALS OF THE QUEEN'S REIGN IN CANADA, 1952-2012

Christopher McCreery

DUNDURN
TORONTO

Editor: Kirk Howard
Copy Editor: Michael Carroll
Design: Jesse Hooper
Printer: Transcontinental

Library and Archives Canada Cataloguing in Publication

McCreery, Christopher
    Commemorative medals of the Queen's reign in Canada, 1952-2012 / Christopher McCreery.

Includes bibliographical references and index.
Issued also in electronic format.
ISBN 978-1-4597-0756-6

    1. Medals--Canada. 2. Elizabeth II, Queen of Great Britain, 1926- --Medals. I. Title.

CJ5823.M32 2012   737'.222   C2012-901424-9

1 2 3 4 5   16 15 14 13 12

We acknowledge the support of the **Canada Council for the Arts** and the **Ontario Arts Council** for our publishing program. We also acknowledge the financial support of the **Government of Canada** through the **Canada Book Fund** and **Livres Canada Books**, and the **Government of Ontario** through the **Ontario Book Publishing Tax Credit** and the **Ontario Media Development Corporation**.

Care has been taken to trace the ownership of copyright material used in this book. The author and the publisher welcome any information enabling them to rectify any references or credits in subsequent editions.

J. Kirk Howard, President

Printed and bound in Canada.
www.dundurn.com

Dundurn	Gazelle Book Services Limited	Dundurn
3 Church Street, Suite 500	White Cross Mills	2250 Military Road
Toronto, Ontario, Canada	High Town, Lancaster, England	Tonawanda, NY
M5E 1M2	LA1 4XS	U.S.A. 14150

In memory of Bruce Wilbur Beatty,
CM, CD, 1922–2011

Her Majesty Queen Elizabeth II, Queen of Canada.

CONTENTS

Diamond Jubilee Emblem.

ACKNOWLEDGEMENTS

T his book marks the 10th such work I have penned about honours and symbols. The collection of colleagues and friends who have assisted and supported my writing about Canadian honours over the past seven years has expanded somewhat with each new publication with the inevitable friendly offers of help and ideas. It should come as no surprise to students of the Canadian honours system that the genesis for this short work came from Major Carl Gauthier, MMM, CD, AdeC. In the weeks leading up to the launch of the diamond jubilee, Gauthier suggested that a short work, modelled on Howard N. Cole's *Coronation and Royal Commemorative Medals, 1887–1977*, be written about the commemorative medals that have been bestowed upon Canadians throughout The Queen's distinguished reign.

Thanks are owed to the Office of the Secretary to the Governor General for providing a number of the images that have been included in this work. Deputy Chief Herald of Canada Bruce Patterson was of great assistance in reviewing the manuscript as was Assiniboine Herald Darrell Kennedy. The author is grateful to the Department of National Defence for its ongoing assistance and support. Graham Glockling, LVO, who was intimately involved in Queen Elizabeth II's Silver Jubilee Medal program, was very helpful with his recollections. Tanya Ursual of Eugene Ursual Military Antiquarian Inc. provided a number of photos in a prompt manner. Rennie Alcock of British

Medals was generous in providing photos related to Victorian jubilee medals. Ed Haynes was helpful with photographs and details related to commemorative medals of India and Pakistan. Lindsay "Bulldog" Drummond was extremely helpful in locating various Cabinet documents and reports in a timely fashion.

A small cadre of other friends supported this project throughout its short period of development, notably Joyce Bryant, CM, BEM; John G. Geiger, FRCGS; Anna Laperle; Alana Blouin; Lieutenant-Commander Scott Nelson, MVO, RCN; Glen Hodgins; and Ray Novak, LVO.

Lastly, I remain grateful to Kirk Howard and Dundurn Press for continuing to support my work on the history and development of Canadian honours and symbols.

Christopher McCreery, MVO
Government House
Halifax, Nova Scotia

PREFACE

With the diamond jubilee of Queen Elizabeth II's accession to the throne, we are provided with an ideal opportunity to survey the history of the commemorative medals that have been issued to Canadians during her reign. This historic moment, the 60th anniversary of a reigning Sovereign's accession, only once before celebrated in the history of Canada, gives us reason to pause and reflect upon the meaning and constancy of these marks of official recognition accorded by Crown and country.

Canada has a long history of employing commemorative medals to recognize civil and military achievement during anniversary years, whether it is a coronation, jubilee of accession, or the anniversary of Confederation. While the history of coronation medallions — medals not intended for wear and generally without ribbons — can be traced back to 1547, the striking and awarding of medals to mark other occasions, such as the anniversary of Canadian Confederation, are a much more recent development. This innovation dates back to the independence of India and Pakistan in 1947 and the creation of commemorative medals to mark the establishment of these two countries as independent members of the Commonwealth during the reign of King George VI. It is fitting that Canada shares this tradition with India and Pakistan given that these two countries have such an enduring relationship with Canada through the Commonwealth connection. In Canada the tradition of commemorative medals has expanded beyond Royal anniversaries and the anniversary of Confederation to include the anniversary of territories entering Confederation as provinces, thereby demonstrating the flexibility and multi-faceted nature of the Canadian honours system.

This short book examines the history and development of official commemorative medals in Canada and places them in the context of not only our national honours system but those of our Commonwealth counterparts. The focus herein is on those commemorative medals that are official honours bestowed by the Crown at the national and provincial levels. The myriad of commemorative medallions (including the 1867 Confederation Medal, 1927 diamond jubilee of Confederation medallion, 1939 Royal Tour medallion, 1953 coronation medallion, and 1977 silver jubilee medallions, the last of the aforementioned five being generously distributed to schoolchildren across the Dominion) bears mentioning but is not the central purpose of this work.

The design, ribbon, manufacture, certificates, and distribution of these medals are examined in detail, with each medal comprising a chapter of this book. It is hoped that a better understanding of the history and development of these honours will enhance the significance and purpose of this often overlooked element of our honours system.

Confederation Medal obverse.   *Confederation Medal reverse.*

INTRODUCTION

While Canada is fortunate to have one of the most comprehensive honours systems in the world, we cannot claim to have invented commemorative medals. As with many of our traditions taken from France and Britain, it will come as no surprise that the tradition of awarding commemorative medals is one that we borrowed from Britain. Yet even the British with their ancient honours system cannot lay claim to creating the first commemorative medals. Credit for this innovation belongs to India's Pudukkottai state, where *khelats* were presented on significant occasions more than half a millennia ago. These *khelats* were not high honours but emblems of recognition, and they served as a mechanism for recognition as well as a means of ensuring stability within the existing order.[1] While the bestowal of commemorative medals may peripherally have this effect today, it is certainly no longer the intention of such awards. They are, in fact, small tokens of thanks given by the sovereign on special occasions to deserving people, both civilian and military. It was not until the coronation of King Edward VI in 1547 that the first coronation medals were distributed in England, and from there the tradition gradually expanded.

The practice of the state awarding official honours in the form of a medal hanging from a ribbon, intended for wear on specific occasions and bestowed with the authority of the Head of State, is one that has spread throughout the world since the reign of Queen Victoria. Not surprisingly, it was following

Victoria's long reign and multiple jubilees that the striking and awarding of commemorative medals became a common practice among the nations of the world.

It is not only coronations and jubilees that have come to be commemorated with the creation of such honours but also the achievement of independence, Confederation, the establishment of a ruling family, the attainment of women's suffrage, and the subsequent anniversaries that have come to be marked with these modern-day *khelats* that are found in many national honours systems.[2] Countries such as Australia, Belgium, Gabon, Ireland, New Zealand, Zambia, and nearly 100 others have issued commemorative medals over the past century. The bestowal of official recognition is a common occurrence in countries around the globe. Honours are not unlike flags, coins, and passports — part of the symbolic equipment that all sovereign states employ alongside the more concrete legal and constitutional entities such as legislative, judicial systems, and military forces.

All of the commemorative medals that are included in the Canadian honours system recognize a coronation, a jubilee of the Sovereign's accession to the throne, or the anniversary of some aspect of Confederation, be it at the national or provincial level.

King Charles II's Coronation Medal obverse.   *King Charles II's Coronation Medal reverse.*

During the reign of our current Queen, for each of these events, with the exception of the coronation in 1953 and the 2012 diamond jubilee, there has been a Royal Tour of Canada by The Queen. The link between the Crown, commemoration, and Royal Tours is one that runs deep.

Ranked near the end of the order of precedence for wearing orders, decorations, and medals, commemorative medals do not have the same allure as the Cross of Valour, the Star of Military Valour, the General Campaign Star for service in Afghanistan, or even the venerable Canadian Forces' Decoration. Obviously, commemorative medals have a more muted significance than those honours at the upper level of our recognition pyramid. That they are generously distributed has occasionally caused some to question their usefulness as "just another medal that comes up with the rations," yet these medals constitute one of the most accessible and participatory elements of our honours system.

Few citizens commit feats of heroism or engage in lifelong endeavours of an exemplary nature that lead to their receiving a decoration for bravery or appointment to the Order of Canada. However, many do render important services to their community, be it at the local, provincial, or national level. Dating back to King George V's Silver Jubilee Medal in 1935, Canadian commemorative medals have long been awarded to those citizens who, on a quiet daily basis, add to the well-being of their fellow humans.

Commemorative medals can also serve as the proverbial stepping stone to more exalted recognition. One illustrative case is that of renowned journalist and author John Fraser. As a reporter, he was awarded the 1967 Centennial Medal at the youthful age of 23. Additional honours have followed over a career that spans fields, continents, and institutions, culminating with his appointment to the Order of Canada 34 years later.

Despite the fact that commemorative medals have less mystique or prestige than our senior national honours, they have great meaning to the recipients, their families, and the communities in that they recognize important services that deserve official acknowledgement — a lasting token of thanks from a grateful Sovereign and country.

I

COMMEMORATIVE MEDALS
THROUGHOUT THE COMMONWEALTH

The first commemorative medals distributed during a coronation came in 1547 to commemorate the coronation of King Edward VI. From the reign of James I, coronation medals were routinely issued to those attending coronation services; by the coronation of James II in 1685, the medals were being issued in gold and silver, with separate medals for The King and Queen.[1] These medals were in reality medallions or commemorative coins not intended for wear. The distribution of medals immediately following a coronation ceremony was not always a happy affair as such events often caused an undignified scramble for souvenirs, what became known as "The King's Princely Largess."[2] The concept of a formalized investiture for coronation medals would not follow for several

Queen Victoria's Coronation Medal obverse.

Queen Victoria's Coronation Medal reverse.

centuries. The practice of distributing such mementos — what have evolved into honours — was discontinued at the corona-tion of King Edward VII.[3] One can imagine the highly amusing scene of the great and the good of the land scrambling for these little silver coins — tangible proof of their participation in the most important state event in the life of the nation.

Queen Victoria in later life.

The British tradition of awarding official commemorative medals — mounted on a ribbon for wear — first emerged with the proclamation of Queen Victoria as Empress of India in 1876 and the resulting celebrations that took place in India on 1 January 1877.

A large medal measuring 58 mm in diameter was produced in gold and silver. Gold medals were awarded to Indian princes and a select number of senior officials, while those in silver were awarded to selected officers and men. The medal was unusually large in size, over 20 mm larger than campaign medals, and the feature that it was to be worn around the neck made it awkward to wear. In addition, those in military uniform were not permitted to wear the insignia. While this was the first wearable commemorative medal instituted in the Commonwealth, the first standardized commemorative medal would come with Queen Victoria's golden jubilee, one decade later.

Queen Victoria's golden jubilee marked only the second time in British history that a monarch had reigned for half a century — the previous occasion being in 1810 during the reign of King George III. This first momentous occasion was marked

Empress of India Medal obverse.   *Empress of India Medal reverse.*

by a service of thanksgiving and fireworks display at Frogmore, but no commemorative medal intended for wear was struck. It is worth noting that the practice of wearing insignia, other than the insignia of orders of chivalry, would not take root until the middle of the nineteenth century, so the concept of a wearable jubilee or coronation medal was simply not considered at this point. To mark the occasion, however, a 44 mm bronze medal was produced depicting an effigy of George III on the obverse and the display of fireworks at the royal residence at Frogmore on the reverse.

In honour of Queen Victoria's golden jubilee in 1887, special wearable medals were produced in gold, silver, and bronze and were awarded to people involved in the jubilee procession and other government officials.[4] In typical Victorian fashion, whether one was awarded the gold, silver, or bronze jubilee medal was dictated by one's social rank. This entire affair was repeated in 1897 for Queen Victoria's diamond jubilee.

When Edward VII acceded to the throne in 1901, a special coronation medal was issued, this time only in silver and bronze and distributed following, not during, the coronation ceremony. The tradition was continued when King George V was crowned in 1911 after he succeeded his father the year before. This time the medal was struck in silver only, and one was not required to participate in the coronation/jubilee procession in order to receive it. Twenty-five years later, when George V celebrated his silver jubilee, another medal was issued — the first silver jubilee medal to be struck. Two more coronation medals were eventually issued — one in 1937 for the coronation of King George VI and the other in 1953 for the coronation of Queen Elizabeth II.

Canadians were eligible for every one of these commemorative medals, although the 1887 Golden Jubilee and 1897 Diamond Jubilee Medals were awarded sparingly, and thus only a few Canadians received them. Most notable among them were Sir John A. Macdonald (1887) and Sir Wilfrid

Laurier (1897). As will be discussed in Chapter 2, since the 1935 silver jubilee, all Canadian commemorative medals have been awarded to a wide cross-section of society and thus there developed a tradition in Canada of not only recognizing senior officials but also recognizing those who make a tangible difference at the local level.

During The Prince of Wales's Royal Tour of Canada in 1860, a bronze medallion was created to commemorate the visit by the future King. A similar medallion was produced for the 1901 visit of the Duke and Duchess of Cornwall and York. These were more souvenirs than awards and were never intended to be worn. In 1868 a special Confederation Medal (not intended for wear) was issued and awarded to the Fathers of Confederation and other dignitaries. While it was a table medal, it was the first uniquely Canadian commemorative medal produced at the direction of the Government of Canada.

Victoria's golden jubilee brought about Empire-wide celebrations. This was in part undertaken to help rehabilitate The Queen's image, which had suffered on account of her near-perpetual state of mourning following the death of her beloved consort Prince Albert in 1861. Celebrations were held around the world, with the main events taking place in London. To commemorate the 50th anniversary of Queen Victoria's accession to the throne, the British government decided to issue a special commemorative medal, the first official wearable jubilee medal issued in the Commonwealth. The noted die engravers J.B. and A.B. Wyon were commissioned to design the medal. This was the first time that a jubilee medal was hung from a ribbon and intended to be worn with military medals. The medal was struck in gold, silver, and bronze.

Gold issues were presented to various members of the Royal Family along with favoured Indian princes. Silver issues were presented to officers and some senior government officials. The bronze issues were reserved for non-commissioned officers and

Queen Victoria's Golden Jubilee Medal obverse. Note the 1897 bar commemorating the Queen's diamond jubilee.

lesser government officials. The medals were primarily presented to those officials who attended the jubilee celebrations in London.

Queen Victoria's Golden Jubilee Medal reverse.

The medal is circular 30 mm in diameter — of bronze, silver, or gold — and depicts a veiled Queen Victoria on the obverse, circumscribed by the text VICTORIA D.G. REGINA ET IMPERATIX. F.D. The reverse depicts a wreath of roses, thistles, and shamrocks, open at the top to include a Royal Crown, and tied at the base by a ribbon. Within the wreath is the text, on eight lines, IN

COMMEMORATION OF THE 50TH YEAR OF THE REIGN OF QUEEN VICTORIA 21 JUNE 1887. The suspender was simple in its construction, consisting of an eyelet screwed into the top of the medal through which passed another ring through which passed the ribbon. The ribbon, like that of all subsequent coronation and jubilee medals (other than special police issues) was 32 mm wide. A total of 361 gold, 1,235 silver, and 5,859 bronze medals were awarded. Only two medals were presented to Canadians, both in silver. Canada did not send a contingent to the golden

jubilee celebrations. This tradition would commence in 1897 with the diamond jubilee of Victoria's accession.

Queen Victoria's diamond jubilee in 1897 resulted in another celebration and yet another jubilee medal. This celebration was truly imperial in its character with contingents

Queen Victoria's Diamond Jubilee Medal obverse.

Queen Victoria's Diamond Jubilee Medal reverse.

gathered from across Britain's far-flung Empire. As with the Golden Jubilee Medal, the Diamond Jubilee Medals were primarily presented to those officials who attended the jubilee celebrations in London. Medals were struck in bronze, silver, and gold. Members of the Canadian contingent were awarded the medal in silver and bronze. These medals were personally presented by The Prince of Wales (the future King Edward VII) at Buckingham Palace on 3 July 1897. The Canadian Militia and North-West Mounted Police were in the final element of the jubilee procession that paraded through London on 22 June. The newly knighted Canadian prime minister, Sir Wilfrid Laurier, also attended the official festivities.

The insignia for the 1897 Diamond Jubilee Medal was identical to that of the 1887 issue with the sole exception of the inscription on the reverse, which now read IN COMMEMORATION OF THE 60TH YEAR OF THE REIGN OF QUEEN VICTORIA 21 JUNE 1897. Recipients of the Golden Jubilee Medal in 1887 who also participated in the diamond jubilee were awarded a bar to their

Canadian Prime Minister Sir Wilfrid Laurier (in landau) during the diamond jubilee procession in London, 22 June 1897.

Golden Jubilee Medal instead of being awarded the Diamond Jubilee Medal. The bar was awarded in the same metal as the original medal. It bore the date *1897* surrounded by a rope and surmounted with a Royal Crown and was sewn onto the ribbon of the recipient's Golden Jubilee Medal.

A total of 73 gold, 3,040 silver, and 890 bronze medals were awarded. Of this the Canadian contingent received 37 silver and 165 bronze medals. An additional 15 medals in silver were awarded to prominent Canadian men of public life.

Montreal shops decorated for Queen Victoria's diamond jubilee.

With the coronation of King Edward VII in 1902 came an even grander affair than what had been staged for his mother's diamond jubilee. Coronation contingents from throughout the Empire gathered in London. The coronation was scheduled to take place on 26 June. However, The King fell ill with appendicitis, and the ceremony was delayed until 9 August. The Canadian delegation, which had arrived on 16 June, returned to Canada on Dominion Day, there having been many complaints among the troops about the lengthy delay. On 25 July a smaller coronation contingent was dispatched, and 633 officers and men of the Canadian Militia and North-West Mounted Police participated in the coronation procession.

King Edward VII's Coronation Medal
in bronze obverse.

King Edward VII's Coronation Medal
in bronze reverse.

The 1902 coronation medal was the first standard-issue coronation medal intended for wear ever awarded. It was primarily presented to those officials who attended the coronation celebrations in London. A circular medal 30 mm in diameter, struck in silver or bronze, its obverse contains the conjoined busts of King Edward VII and Queen Alexandra, both crowned and wearing their coronation robes, surrounded by a thin border of laurel leaves and surmounted by a Tudor Crown. The reverse contains the Royal Cypher and the date 26 JUNE 1902. While this was not the actual date of the coronation, the medals had already been struck and were issued with the original coronation date on the reverse. For the suspender a small ring was attached to the Crown on the top of the medal through which the ribbon passes. The ribbon is dark blue, 32 mm wide, is edged with 2 mm of white, and bears in the centre a 7 mm wide red stripe. A total of 3,494 silver and 6,054 bronze medals were issued. Canadians received 25 silver and 608 bronze medals. They were presented to members of the coronation contingent by Edward VII in the gardens of Buckingham Palace on 11 August.

King Edward VII's coronation day celebrations, His Majesty's Dockyard Halifax, 9 August 1902.

Following the tradition established by King Edward VII, a special coronation medal was issued to commemorate the coronation of King George V in 1911. This was the first coronation/jubilee medal issue in which the standard medal was struck in silver alone. Thus, non-commissioned officers, officers, and princes all received the same medal. Primarily bestowed upon participants in the coronation contingent, a number were also awarded to senior government officials.

The Commemorative Medal for the Coronation of King George V is a circular silver medal, 32 mm in diameter. The obverse depicts the conjoined busts of King George V and Queen Mary, both crowned and wearing their coronation robes, surrounded by a floral wreath. The reverse has a beaded border and is plain, bearing only the Royal Cypher of King George V and the date 22 JUNE 1911. The suspender consists of a small eyelet screwed into the top of the medal through which

King George V's Coronation Medal obverse.

King George V's Coronation Medal reverse.

Portage Avenue, Winnipeg, decoration for King George V's coronation.

The Canadian Contingent at King George V's coronation in London, England.

passes another larger ring that is suspended from the ribbon. The ribbon is blue, 32 mm wide, and defaced in the centre by two 2 mm red stripes, 1 mm apart.

In total, 15,901 medals were struck for award throughout the Empire, of which 1,007 were awarded to Canadians. On coronation day Canadians lined the procession route in London and also provided a mounted squadron for the parade. For the royal procession through London, held the day after the coronation, Canada provided a small mounted escort of four officers and 24 soldiers. The balance of the Canadian contingent lined the processional route. The King presented medals to the Canadians at Buckingham Palace on 30 June. The contingent of 827 Canadians included members of the Canadian Militia, the Royal North-West Mounted Police, and 38 personnel from the newly established Royal Canadian Navy.

Besides the standard-issue medals described above, for every one of these Royal occasions from 1887 to 1911 there were also special issues struck in different designs and metals for members of various British police services, fire brigades, St. John Ambulance, and other quasi-governmental organizations, mostly associated with security for these major events. Starting with the 1935 Silver Jubilee Medal, there was only one standard issue for all recipients, regardless of whether they were civilian,

Painting of the Canadian Contingent at King George V's coronation in London.

Queen Victoria's Diamond Jubilee Medal for mayors and provosts.

military, or police. The British also awarded special mayors and provosts medals for the 1897 diamond jubilee and the 1902 coronation. No Canadian mayor received these medals as they were reserved for officials in the United Kingdom only.

In addition to the various jubilee and coronation medals mentioned in this chapter, commemorative medals were also awarded on the occasion of the Delhi Durbar in 1903 and in 1911 when Edward VII and George V were respectively crowned Emperor of India. In 1910 the newly formed Union of South Africa issued the Union of South Africa Medal to commemorate the establishment of that country. The Union of South Africa Medal was in essence the first in a long series of independence medals issued throughout the Commonwealth. Visits to Ireland made by Queen Victoria in 1900, in 1903 by King Edward VII, and in 1911 by King George V were also commemorated with official commemorative

King Edward VII's Delhi Durbar Medal obverse.

King Edward VII's Delhi Durbar Medal reverse.

medals. These were awarded to members of the Royal Irish Constabulary and Dublin Metropolitan Police who were on duty during the visit. The criteria for the 1911 Visit to Ireland Medal also included senior civic and government officials. King Edward VII's post-coronation tour of Scotland resulted in a similar medal in 1903. The King's Visit to Scotland Medal was awarded to police involved in the visit, along with members of the Fire Brigade and St. Andrew's Ambulance Association.

Other parts of the Commonwealth and Empire struck their own medals to mark jubilees and coronations, but these were never officially sanctioned for wear. Among the most impressive were Queen Victoria's Diamond Jubilee Medal and King Edward VII's Coronation Medal struck by the Government of Ceylon

Queen Victoria's Diamond Jubilee Medal Ceylon issue obverse.

Queen Victoria's Diamond Jubilee Medal Ceylon issue reverse.

(modern-day Sri Lanka). These medals were produced in 14 carat gold and silver and were awarded to senior government officials and local leaders. While no awards of these medals were made to people living in Canada, they do provide an idea of the context in which jubilee and commemorative medals developed.

Aside from war medals awarded for service in the First and Second World Wars, it was coronation and jubilee medals that first introduced many Canadians to the honours system as many ordinary citizens received such recognition, beginning with King George V's Silver Jubilee Medal and continuing to this day. These were also the first medals to be awarded in great number to women.

The tradition established in 1887 with the striking of Queen Victoria's Golden Jubilee Medal is one that continues to be observed in Canada. Indeed, from the 1953 Queen Elizabeth II's Coronation Medal to the newly minted Queen Elizabeth II's Diamond Jubilee Medal, the convention of bestowing commemorative medals on a broad cross-section of citizenry has become an important part of the Canadian honours system. That these awards continue to serve as Royal favours predominantly used to reward citizens who have made a significant contribution at the local level is a testament to how "Canadianized" they have become.

2

1935 Jubilee and 1937 Coronation — Setting the Pattern

T he silver jubilee of King George V's accession to the throne brought about the first issue of a jubilee medal for a silver anniversary. London saw a magnificent series of jubilee-related events, including a service of thanksgiving, a parade, and a naval review. Canada was represented by a contingent from the Royal Canadian Navy, the Canadian Army, the Royal Canadian Air Force, and the Royal Canadian Mounted Police. In Canada The King's jubilee was marked by a national holiday with celebrations and parades in many communities. There was also an address by The King to the entire Commonwealth and Empire. The Royal Canadian Mint struck the first circulation silver dollar, while the Bank of Canada printed a special $25 bill and the sentence of federal prisoners was reduced to mark the event.

The 25th anniversary of The King's accession to the throne resulted in celebrations being held throughout the Commonwealth and Empire to mark his dedication and service. Included in the celebrations was the first widely distributed commemorative medal that was given to a much more diverse array of citizens than had been recognized with commemorative medals in the past. Up until the 1935 silver jubilee, as was customary throughout the Commonwealth, most commemorative medals had been awarded to members of the military and senior state officials who had some involvement with the actual ceremonial event. In Canada the distribution of the 1911 Commemorative Medal for the Coronation of King George V saw 1,007 Canadians recognized, of whom 719 recipients were members of the Canadian military and the Royal North-West Mounted Police who had attended the coronation. The balance included Canadian militia officers and senior federal government officials. It was a limited distribution that focused on those who attended the coronation and those who served in some Crown office in Canada.

Unlike previous coronation and jubilee medal programs, the number of medals struck for the 1935 silver jubilee well outstripped those who had a direct involvement in the actual jubilee procession and ceremonies. Of the 85,235 medals struck, Canada was allotted 7,500 medals by the Dominions Office, which used a population-based formula to determine the distribution of medals among the Dominions and colonies. The generous offering of medals to Canada coincided with a change in honours policy that had been instituted by Prime Minister R.B. Bennett.

King George V's Silver Jubilee Medal obverse.

King George V's Silver Jubilee Medal reverse.

Toward the end of the First World War, the nation had been gripped by debate over honours and titles, specifically the bestowal of peerages on Canadians and the perception that honours such as peerages and knighthoods were being bought and sold. This resulted in the adoption of the Nickle Resolution and the *Report of the Special Committee on Honours and Titles 1919*, which saw the flow of honours in post-war Canada come to an end. Liberal and Conservative politicians refused to re-examine the issue until R.B. Bennett was elected prime minister in 1930.

BUCKINGHAM PALACE.

By Command

of

HIS MAJESTY THE KING

the accompanying Medal is forwarded

to

MR. F. L. C. PEREIRA   O.B.E.

to be worn in commemoration of

Their Majesties' Silver Jubilee

6th May, 1935.

King George V's Silver Jubilee Medal certificate.

Silver Jubilee Medal transmittal box (gentleman's version).

During his five years in office, Bennett reintroduced honours in Canada and recommended 18 knighthoods and 151 appointments to the civil division of the Order of the British Empire. Notable Canadians such as Sir Frederick Banting, the co-discoverer of insulin, Lucy Maud Montgomery, author of the Anne of Green Gables books, musician Sir Ernest MacMillan, and a young diplomat named Lester B. Pearson were all recognized by the Crown with honours during this period. Seventy-seven of the Canadian appointments to the Order of the British Empire were women working in a variety of fields, mainly volunteer-based or social services focusing on Depression relief efforts. Gone were the days of honours as patronage tools, as Bennett promoted the idea of honours as a mechanism to recognize good works at the community level — what today we would characterize as exemplary citizenship.

These awards were among the most diverse and representative of Canadian society that would be made until the establishment of the Order of Canada in 1967. The desire to recognize citizens who made a contribution to Canadian society at the local level, and in hitherto unrecognized fields, dovetailed nicely with the Silver Jubilee Medal program. To a lesser degree the bestowal of the Silver Jubilee Medal in Britain, Australia, New Zealand, and India went beyond the narrow caste of senior officials, brass hats, and members of the military. In Canada it was this silver jubilee that initiated the tradition of involving local representatives, non-governmental organizations, and parliamentarians in the selection of recipients for commemorative medals.

The 1935 medal was awarded to Canadians in recognition of their participation in the official silver jubilee celebrations held in London. Recipients also included those selected by senior government officials, senators, or members of Parliament, as having performed valuable services to the community or Canada as a whole. A variety of non-governmental organizations, including St. John Ambulance, YMCA, YWCA, Red Cross, Victorian Order of Nurses, Imperial Order of the Daughters of the Empire, and various relief organizations, were allotted medals for their employees and volunteers. A number of groups that had been previously excluded from the honours system, notably the Inuit and other Native peoples, were now included in the awards made, and nearly 20 percent of the Silver Jubilee Medals went to women. The most notable Inuit recipient of the medal was Stephen Angulalik, a storyteller, photographer, and fur trader who also went on to earn Queen Elizabeth II's Coronation Medal.

Members of the Royal Canadian Navy, the Canadian Army, and the Royal Canadian Air Force received 1,154 medals, with the balance being awarded to civilians and a small number to the Royal Canadian Mounted Police. All living holders of the Victoria Cross were awarded the medal, initiating a tradition that VC holders receive every commemorative medal issued during their lifetime. Awards made to Canadians were published in the *Canada Gazette* on 4 May 1935.

The Silver Jubilee Medal is silver, 32 mm in diameter, and was struck by the Royal Mint. The obverse bears the conjoined busts of King George V and Queen Mary, both crowned and wearing their coronation robes, circumscribed by the text GEORGE V AND QUEEN MARY MAY VI MCMXXXV. The reverse contains the Royal Arms and the dates MAY 6 1910–MAY 6 1935. Designed by Sir William Goscombe, this was the second commemorative medal, after the Union of South Africa Medal, to be fitted with a claw-footed suspender. The ribbon is a dark red, 32 mm in width, edged on each side by 1 mm blue, 2 mm white, and 1 mm blue stripes. The medal was issued in a red cardboard transmittal box with flip-lid opening sideways, impressed with a black Tudor Crown and the dates *1910–1935*. Recipients also received a certificate bearing their name (type-written or in calligraphy) on watermarked paper, bearing the Royal Arms embossed in red at the top of the page. A total of 85,324 medals were awarded to people throughout the Commonwealth and Empire.

King George V died on 20 January 1936 after more than a quarter-century on the throne and was succeeded by his eld-est son, Edward, The Prince of Wales, who took the style King

King George V and Queen Mary receiving loyal addresses from the House of Lords, the House of Commons, and the Dominions, 9 May 1935.

Edward VIII. Coronation day was set for 12 May 1937. The young King, however, had fallen in love with Wallis Simpson, an American divorcée, and ultimately decided to marry her, giving up the throne for the woman he loved. King Edward VIII's younger brother, Albert, The Duke of York, acceded to the throne as King George VI on 11 December 1936. The coronation plans that were already in the works continued, with George VI and Queen Elizabeth substituted as the principals.

Governor General Lord Bessborough presiding over the inaugural investiture on Parliament Hill, 1935.

Coronation Day in 1937 was a magnificent affair, and Canada was represented by 351 officers, men and women of the Royal Canadian Navy, the Canadian Army, the Royal Canadian Air Force, and the Royal Canadian Mounted Police. Several days before, on 9 May, Canadians joined their Commonwealth counterparts in serving sentry duty outside Buckingham Palace, the first time in history that Commonwealth troops had done so. On 14 May, George VI reviewed the Commonwealth contingents and

King George VI's coronation, 1937.

King George VI and Prime Minister William Lyon Mackenzie King enjoying a lighter moment during the Commonwealth Conference that followed the 1937 coronation.

presented 1,200 Coronation Medals. Canada was also represented at the coronation by a party of senior officials, including Prime Minister William Lyon Mackenzie King. Meanwhile, in Ottawa, Lord Tweedsmuir, the governor general, presided over a national ceremony in Ottawa marking the occasion.

The criteria used for Canadian recipients of the Commemorative Medal for the Coronation of King George VI were the same as that employed for the Commemorative Medal for the Silver Jubilee of King George V. The program was administered by the Department of the Secretary of State, which had not two years before been in charge of the Canadian distribution of Sil-

ver Jubilee Medals. A total of 10,359 medals were awarded to Canadians, with 1,284 medals going to members of the military. Throughout the Commonwealth and Empire a total of 90,279 Coronation Medals were bestowed.

King George VI's Coronation Medal obverse.

King George VI's Coronation Medal reverse.

44

The 32 mm silver medal was struck by the Royal Mint. Designed by Percy Metcalfe, the obverse bears conjoined busts of King George VI and Queen Elizabeth, crowned and wearing their coronation robes. The reverse is defaced by the Royal Cypher in the centre with the text CROWNED 12 MAY 1937 below, and circumscribed by the text GEORGE VI QUEEN ELIZABETH. The suspender is identical to that used on the Silver Jubilee Medal, while the ribbon is blue, 32 mm wide, edged on each side by stripes of 1 mm white, 2 mm red, and 1 mm white.

BUCKINGHAM PALACE.

By Command

of

HIS MAJESTY THE KING

the accompanying Medal is forwarded

to

MR. F.L.C. PEREIRA, O.B.E.

to be worn in commemoration of

Their Majesties' Coronation

12th May, 1937.

King George VI's Coronation Medal certificate.

The medal was issued in a rectangular red cardboard transmittal box, with a flip lid opening sideways. On the lid was printed in black the Royal Cypher separating the coronation year digits *19* and *37*, with the inscription CORONATION MEDAL in a semicircle below. The medal was originally designed to bear the bust of King Edward VIII, but following his abdication the design was hastily changed. Recipients also received a certificate bearing their name (typewritten or in calligraphy) on watermarked paper, with the Royal Cypher embossed in red at the top of the page.

Coronation Medal transmittal box (lady's version).

3

QUEEN ELIZABETH II'S CORONATION, 1953

The accession and subsequent coronation of Queen Elizabeth II marked the first time that the Sovereign's style and title officially included reference to Canada, for Elizabeth II became Canada's Head of State as Queen of Canada and the new designation was formalized with the *Royal Style and Titles Act, 1953*. While The Queen's father, King George VI, his brother, King Edward VIII, and their father, King George V, had all been, in legal fact, "Kings of Canada," their official title did not reflect that fact. This development came about with the passage of the *Statute of Westminster* in 1931, which gave Canada autonomy over its own affairs and recognized the Dominion of Canada as being a separate legal entity from the United Kingdom. Yet it was not until 1953 that our Sovereign's title was changed to reflect this new Canadian reality. Until the reign of Queen Elizabeth II, Canada, along with Australia, New Zealand, South Africa, Pakistan, and Ceylon, had simply been included in the Royal style and title as "the British Dominions beyond the seas." This practice had begun with the reign of King Edward VII.

In October 1951, Princess Elizabeth and her husband, The Duke of Edinburgh, embarked upon an extensive Royal Tour of Canada, visiting every province in the Dominion and concluding their 33-day trip in the newest province, Newfoundland, on 12 November. Eighty-six days later Princess Elizabeth became Queen of Canada.

The Queen's wearing of multiple Crowns — in a legal, not physical sense — was perhaps best illustrated in her coronation oath given on 2 June 1953:

> **Archbishop:** Madam, is Your Majesty willing to take the Oath?
>
> **Queen:** I am willing.
>
> **Archbishop:** Will you solemnly promise and swear to govern the Peoples of the United Kingdom of Great Britain and Northern Ireland, Canada, Australia, New Zealand, the Union of South Africa, Pakistan and Ceylon, and your Possessions and other Territories to any of them belong or pertaining according to their respective laws and customs?
>
> **Queen:** I do solemnly promise so to do.

The coronation ceremony did not take place until 2 June 1953, more than a year following the death of King George VI. This was in part to observe a period of mourning, Commonwealth-wide, and also because Britain was still feeling the effects of the Second World War. The rationing of certain items and austerity measures persisted well beyond the end of the Second World War, resulting in limited resources.

Every part of the Commonwealth was represented at the coronation. Canada's official delegation to the coronation included Prime Minister Louis St. Laurent and five members of the federal Cabinet, including the leader of the government in the Senate, the chief justice of Canada, and the leaders of Her Majesty's Loyal Opposition from the Senate and the House of Commons. The speakers of both houses of Parliament, the Canadian high commissioner to London, the undersecretary of state, and their respective spouses also attended. Canadian officials joined representatives from throughout the Commonwealth, filling

Westminster Abbey with 7,000 guests. The parade route was lined with soldiers, sailors, airmen, and airwomen from around the Commonwealth who participated in events before and after the actual coronation ceremony.

Canada sent the largest contingent it had ever dispatched to London for a ceremonial occasion. It was also one of the largest of the Commonwealth delegations to participate in the coronation. A total of 856 officers, servicemen, and servicewomen

Parliament Hill on coronation day, 2 June 1953.

participated in the celebrations, with representation from the Royal Canadian Navy, the Canadian Army, the Royal Canadian Air Force, and the Royal Canadian Mounted Police. The Royal 22nd Regiment band provided the Canadian musical component for the coronation parade, while "O Lord Our Governor," written by Canadian organist Healey Willan, was played during the coronation ceremony itself.

In honour of coronation day, Governor General Vincent Massey proclaimed a national holiday, and ceremonies were held across Canada. The national celebrations focused on Parliament Hill where Massey presided over the festivities. At 3:45 p.m. that day the governor general arrived on Parliament Hill and alighted, inspected the guard, and then ascended a platform erected in front of the Peace Tower. Here Massey spoke to the assembled tens of thousands, and his address of loyalty to the new Sovereign was broadcast across the country in both official languages. The governor general's flag was then lowered from

Canadian Contingent in the coronation parade, 2 June 1953, London.

the Peace Tower, and the Royal Standard was raised in its place simultaneous with a fanfare of trumpets. The governor general then proudly announced "Her Majesty The Queen," and The Queen's coronation speech was then rebroadcast. At the conclusion of the broadcast there was a call for three cheers for The Queen followed by the massed bands playing "O Canada" and "God Save The Queen." The Royal Standard was then replaced by the governor general's flag, and the last notes of "God Save The Queen" were marked by a flypast of the Royal Canadian Air Force and the firing of a 42-gun salute. The national ceremony concluded with a march past of troops before a reviewing stand placed in front of the Parliament Buildings. That evening a concert was offered to the general public on Parliament Hill, while the governor general hosted a state ball at Rideau Hall. A special coronation garden party was subsequently held on June 6.

In addition to the Commemorative Medal for the Coronation of Queen Elizabeth II, the Government of Canada commissioned a coronation medallion that was presented to every schoolchild in Canada. Three million coronation medallions were struck in bronze by the Royal Canadian Mint, the obverse bearing a crowned effigy of The Queen and the reverse displaying the Royal Cypher atop the word CANADA circumscribed by the text ELIZABETH II REGINA CORONATA MCMLIII.

Canada was not involved in the design of Queen Elizabeth II's Coronation Medal, although it did participate fully in the program from its inception in mid-1952. The Coronation Medal program was officially announced by the British Prime Minister's Office on 30 April 1953, following consultations with various Commonwealth prime ministers.

Queen Elizabeth II's Coronation Medal followed the tradition of awarding a special commemorative medal to civilians and members of the armed forces on the occasion of a coronation or jubilee. Many participants in the coronation ceremonies and related events, such as the Naval Review at Spithead in

Hampshire, received the medal. Others were selected by senior government officials, senators, or members of Parliament, for having performed valuable services to the community or Canada as a whole. The focus was on those who had a direct connection with serving the Crown; 5,700 medals went to members of the Royal Canadian Navy, the Canadian Army, and the Royal Canadian Air Force, while 2 percent of federal civil servants received the medal with distribution organized on a departmental basis. All Aboriginal band chiefs were awarded the medal, and a special allotment was set aside for the Inuit. At the municipal level small communities with populations under 1,500 were allotted one medal, while larger communities received

Queen Elizabeth II's Coronation Medal obverse.

Queen Elizabeth II's Coronation Medal reverse.

medals according to a pro-rated population formula. Lieutenant governors received a pro-rated allotment of medals for distribution within their households. All living recipients of the Victoria Cross and George Cross as well as former provincial premiers were awarded the medal.

The issue of the Coronation Medal was repeatedly discussed by the federal Cabinet members. So enamoured were they with the newfound power to distribute honours that they requested 20,000 medals for the Dominion. Ultimately, 19,000 were awarded to Canadians out of the 129,051 distributed throughout the Commonwealth. The overall plan to distribute the medals in Canada was devised by Major-General H.F.G. Letson, CB, DSO, MC, ED, CD, who had recently served as secretary to the governor general and was intimately involved in the creation of the Canadian Forces' Decoration several years before.

Letson took the distribution formula used for King George VI's Coronation Medal and greatly improved it, developing a highly refined distribution that sought to recognize people at all levels of Canadian society, and driven by his commitment that there be "an equitable distribution which will make Queen Elizabeth's Coronation Medal long and well remembered in Canada."[1] A veteran of the First and Second World Wars who had been decorated on several occasions for bravery and meritorious service, Letson insisted "The Coronation Medal should be awarded on the basis of merit."[2] The Letson approach to commemorative medals continues to be a central element of the criteria and distribution formula used to this day.

The medal itself was struck in silver by the Royal Mint and is 32 mm in diameter. Designed by sculptor Cecil Thomas, the obverse depicts a crowned bust of The Queen wearing the collar of the Order of the Garter and the badge of the Order of the Bath. The reverse displays the Royal Cypher circumscribed with the text QUEEN ELIZABETH II CROWNED 2ND JUNE 1953. Following the precedent set by the 1935 Silver Jubilee and 1937 Coronation

Medals, Queen Elizabeth II's Coronation Medal is hung from a claw-footed suspender mounted on top of the medal, through which passes a silver ring and the ribbon. The 32 mm wide ribbon is dark red in colour, edged with 2 mm of white. In the centre a 2 mm line of red is flanked by two 3 mm stripes of blue.

BUCKINGHAM PALACE

By Command of

HER MAJESTY THE QUEEN

the accompanying Medal is forwarded to

Mrs. LILY C.A. BELL.

to be worn in commemoration of

Her Majesty's Coronation

2nd June, 1953

Queen Elizabeth II's Coronation Medal certificate.

The medal was enclosed in a red rectangular transmittal box, with a flip lid opening sideways. On the lid was printed in black the Royal Cypher separating the coronation year digits *19* and *53*, with the inscription CORONATION MEDAL in a semicircle below. Ladies received their medal in a box similar in style but square in shape, which had an additional compartment containing a ready-made bow of the ribbon to which the medal could be sewn for wear after the presentation. Instructions to that effect were printed inside the lid of the box. Recipients also received a certificate bearing their name (typewritten or in calligraphy) on watermarked paper bearing the Royal Cypher embossed in red at the top of the page.

Our newly crowned Queen presented 2,500 Coronation Medals to her troops from throughout the Commonwealth the day after the coronation. It is believed that this remains a record for numbers of medals personally presented by the Sovereign on any single occasion.

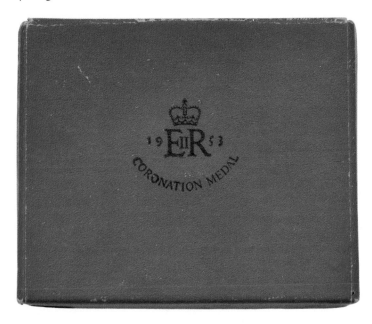

Coronation Medal transmittal box (lady's version).

DISTRIBUTION OF THE COMMEMORATIVE MEDAL
FOR THE CORONATION OF HER MAJESTY QUEEN ELIZABETH II

Group	Number	Total
Those in the Table of Precedence	1 each	969
Governor General's List	160	160
Lieutenant Governors and Staff		79
Prime Minister's Staff		5
Cabinet Ministers' Lists		40
Holders of VC and GC		*
Yukon Territory and Indians		57
Rail and Air Transportation Services		95
National Organizations		1,425
Federal Civil Service		2,409
Crown Corporations, Commissions, and Boards		380
Canadian Diplomats		95
Provincial Public Services		953
Education		1,615
Municipal Officials (allocated depending on population)		2,098
Canadian Armed Forces		5,700
Merchant Navy		76
Police (Provincial and Municipal)		330
Firemen		178
Royal Canadian Mounted Police		230
Civil Defence		38
Veterans' Organizations		1,520
Reserve (extra medals for special issue and for use as replacements)		548
TOTAL		**19,000**

* Living Victoria Cross and George Cross holders were awarded the medal out of the U.K. Privy Purse Allocation. In 1953 Canada had 35 living recipients of the Victoria Cross and two living recipients of the George Cross. Of the VC recipients, George Pearkes received his Coronation Medal as a member of Parliament, while Milton Gregg received his as a member of the Privy Council, bringing the Canadian total of VC and GC recipients awarded the

medal under the U.K. Privy Purse Allocation to 35. It is interesting to note that among the VC recipients, Sir Richard Turner, VC, KCB, KCMG, DSO, had earned his VC more than half a century prior to The Queen's coronation while serving in the South Africa War, 1899–1902.

4

CENTENNIAL OF CONFEDERATION, 1967

The centennial of Canadian Confederation remains the largest party the nation has ever held. Preparation for the "Centennial," as it would become known, began in November 1959 when provincial premiers were invited to nominate representatives to participate in the planning of the event. This was followed by the adoption of the *National Centennial Act*, which came into law in 1961. The act paved the way for the planning of the national celebrations. Years of preparations went into the events that took place across Canada during 1967 to celebrate the founding of Canada. These celebrations were launched on 1 January 1967 when Prime Minister Lester Pearson lit the centennial flame in front of Parliament. Events were held in every part of the country, but the most significant festivities were held in Ottawa and at Expo 67 in Montreal.

During a six-day tour that commenced on 29 June 1967, Her Majesty The Queen and His Royal Highness The Duke of Edinburgh attended Expo, where they toured the various pavilions, before proceeding to Ottawa. On Dominion Day in the nation's capital, Her Majesty presided over an extensive program and military parade, in addition to cutting a massive centennial cake. It was also on this occasion that The Queen invested Governor General Roland Michener as the first Companion of the newly created Order of Canada.

Throughout the Commonwealth there was a tradition of bestowing commemorative medals on the occasion of coronations, jubilees, and other significant national events. When the Union of South Africa was established in 1910, the Union of South Africa Medal was struck to mark the occasion and presented to dignitaries and senior military leaders in very limited number. Subsequently, other non-Royal anniversaries were commemorated with medals, notably the India Independence Medal and the Pakistan Independence Medal. Both were sanctioned by King George VI and awarded respectively to members of the Indian and Pakistani armed forces when their countries became Dominions in 1947.

Union of South Africa Medal obverse.   *Union of South Africa Medal reverse.*

India Independence Medal 1947 obverse.

India Independence Medal 1947 reverse.

Pakistan Independence Medal 1947 obverse.

Pakistan Independence Medal 1947 reverse.

Following the end of the Korean War, the awarding of honours, other than for bravery and long service, came to an effective end for all Canadians. From 1953 until 1967, members of the Royal Canadian Navy, the Canadian Army, and the Royal Canadian Air Force could only expect to receive the Canadian Forces' Decoration or the occasional United Nations service medal. There were virtually no new ribbons to be found on the chests of Canadian servicemen and servicewomen. Proposals for new service medals were regularly submitted to the Department of National Defence, but nothing came of them in large part on account of resistance from civilian officials to expanding the Canadian honours system.

As early as 1961, the Department of National Defence received and began to examine proposals to create a medal to commemorate the centennial of Confederation. The initial proposal called for a medal to be awarded to members of the military as well as to civilians in recognition of their "outstanding contribution to our country."[1] By the middle of 1962, a number of proposals were being developed for a centennial medal. Brigadier H.A. Phillips, director general of army personnel, wrote to the Armed Forces Council that "medals have been instituted to commemorate other such events such as visits by the Sovereign, the union of states and granting of independence."[2]

The concept behind the Centennial Medal was initiated by the Department of National Defence in co-operation with the Office of the Secretary of State beginning with a formal proposal from Undersecretary of State Jean Miquelon in 1963. It was not until 22 January 1964 that the minister of national defence, the newly appointed Paul Hellyer, approved of the project and submitted it to Cabinet for discussion. In May 1965, Hellyer and Secretary of State Maurice Lamontagne made a presentation to Cabinet, recommending the creation of the Centennial Medal as part of the nationwide celebrations planned for 1967. They noted that it would be "a most appropriate occasion for the Government of Canada to recognize the specially valuable service of many Canadian citizens [...] Therefore Her Majesty be graciously pleased to approve the institution of a Canadian medal to commemorate the 100th Anniversary of the Confederation of Canada."[3]

The medal was approved by The Queen on 27 June 1966, four months before a detailed proposal for the establishment of the Order of Canada was actually completed and presented to Cabinet. The announcement of the commemorative medal in a press release from Prime Minister Lester Pearson on 31 May 1967 initially created some confusion between the recently announced Order of Canada and the new Centennial Medal. The press release explained that the Centennial Medal was going to be conferred on "Canadians selected from all sections of Canadian society, including federal, provincial and municipal public services, the military, national associations, industry, labour, education, science and the arts."[4] The medal program was expanded to include veterans' organizations that had been omitted from the original plan, despite having been active partners in the previous commemorative medal programs of 1935, 1937, and 1953. At one point the Department of National Defence proposed that every member of the Canadian Armed Forces who had served five years with honourable conduct be automatically awarded the medal. This proposal was promptly rejected: "It is clearly undesirable to increase the total number of medals to be distributed to such an extent that they would no longer be meaningful as a recognition of valuable service."[5]

The design of the medal, specifically the 1960s angular style suspender, makes the Centennial Medal one of the more unique designs of insignia among Commonwealth commemorative medals. A total of 29,500 medals were awarded in 1967 and into 1968, with the first medals being delivered in August 1967. All living recipients of the Victoria Cross and George Cross were awarded the medal, along with 8,500 members of the Canadian

Forces. Nominations for civilians were made by senators, members of Parliament, premiers, federal government departments, Crown corporations, various national non-governmental organizations, and municipal councils across Canada.

The circular silver medal, 36 mm in diameter, bears a stylized maple leaf superimposed with the Royal Cypher and circumscribed with the words CONFEDERATION CANADA CONFÉDÉRATION on the obverse. The maple leaf takes the same form as that appearing on the new maple leaf flag adopted in 1965. The reverse depicts the Royal Arms of Canada, as rendered by Alan Beddoe, OC, OBE, in 1957, with the dates *1867–1967* in the base. The medal was struck from sterling silver by the Royal Canadian Mint and

was issued unnamed, although those personally presented by the governor general and those awarded to Government House staff members were officially impressed in block capitals with the person's full

*Centennial of Confederation
Commemorative Medal obverse.*

*Centennial of Confederation
Commemorative Medal reverse.*

name (e.g., ESMOND BUTLER). The suspender is a straight bar with angled arms through which passes the ribbon. The ribbon is 32 mm wide, with 5 mm of red on either edge and four equally spaced 1 mm stripes of red set against a white background. The red edges refer to the newly adopted national flag, while the four

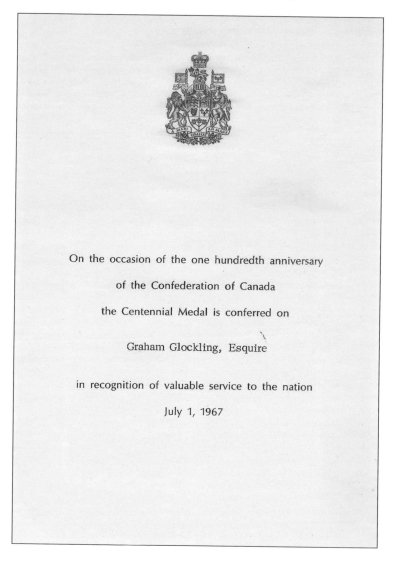

On the occasion of the one hundredth anniversary

of the Confederation of Canada

the Centennial Medal is conferred on

Graham Glockling, Esquire

in recognition of valuable service to the nation

July 1, 1967

Centennial of Confederation Commemorative Medal certificate.

Centennial Medal transmittal case.

thin red stripes each represent a quarter-century of Canadian history since Confederation. Red and white are the official colours of Canada as sanctioned by King George V when he granted the Royal Arms in Right of Canada in 1921.

The concept for the medal and ribbon was devised by Warrant Officer 1st Class Harold A. Diceman. Directions were then given to Bruce Beatty, CM, CD, in March 1965, then with the Graphic Arts Section at National Defence, to create the artwork. Diceman had also suggested a second design option,

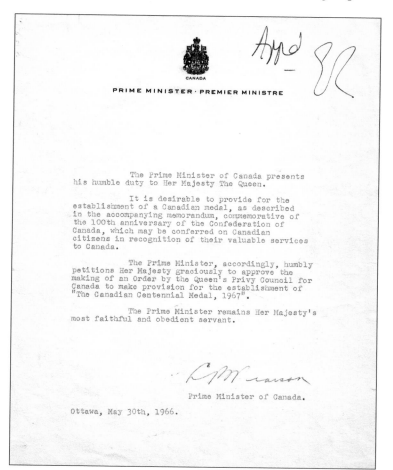

Instrument of Advice creating the Centennial Medal.

which would have replaced the maple leaf and the Royal Cypher on the obverse with The Queen's effigy, as used on Canadian coinage from 1965 to 1989. An early proposal also called for a complicated heavily embroidered ribbon of red, white, and blue decorated with maple leaves.

Standard royal commemorative medals are on a ring suspension, and since 1911, have consistently been 32 mm in diameter, making them visually distinct from campaign and service medals, which have traditionally been 36 mm in diameter with straight suspensions. The Centennial Medal, however, was the first Canadian commemorative medal to take on the appearance of a campaign medal. The reason behind this choice is not known, but it may be that the designers took their inspiration from some recent "constitutional" commemorative medals such as those for the independence of India, Pakistan, and Nigeria. This aspect of the Centennial Medal design was repeated in 1992 for the 125th anniversary of Confederation.

The Centennial Medal was presented in a brown leatherette-covered metal case, its lid stamped with the Royal Arms of Canada in gold (the same case used for the Canadian Forces' Decoration,

Expo 67 postcard.

known as the Farrington box).[6] The medal was also accompanied by two undress ribbon bars. Several gold-plated specimens exist that were originally to be awarded to the Expo 67 commissioners, although there is no evidence that the awards were ever presented.

The medal was issued with a certificate printed on white bond paper with the Royal Arms of Canada in red at the top and the name of the recipient typed below. Certificates were issued in either English or French. In the mid-1990s the Chancellery

Queen Elizabeth II cutting the centennial cake on Dominion Day 1967.

of Honours ran out of the original issue of the Centennial Medal struck by the Royal Canadian Mint. The contract to strike replacement issues was then awarded to Henry Birks & Sons. The Birks issues, although produced in sterling silver, are distinguishable from the mint's original striking because they are slightly thinner and the upper bar on the reverse of the suspender is marked BIRKS STERLING in raised letters.

Distribution of Canadian Centennial Medal

Group	Number	Total
Those in the Table of Precedence*	1 each	2,000
Governor General's List		160
Lieutenant Governors and Staff	6 per province	60
Prime Minister's Staff		280
Cabinet Ministers' Lists		
Centennial Officials		
Expo 67 Officials		
Holders of VC and GC		†
Indians		275
Yukon Territory and Northwest Territories	30 to Inuit 30 to non-Inuit	60
National Organizations		1,500
Federal Civil Service		3,000
Provincial Lists		4,500
Provincial Judges and Magistrates		150
Education	12 medals per 1,000 teachers	2,400
Municipal Officials (allocated depending on population)		4,150
Canadian Armed Forces		8,500
Royal Canadian Mounted Police		275
Veterans' Organizations		2,000

Reserve (extra medals for special issue and for use as replacements)		190
TOTAL		29,500

* This included list was expanded to also include former premiers, chief officers of the public service, deputy ministers, members of government boards, and diplomatic and trade missions lists.

† Those recipients of the VC and GC who were living as of 1 July 1967 were awarded the medal out of the veterans' category.

Queen Elizabeth II and Governor General Roland Michener following the conclusion of The Queen's 1967 Centennial Visit.

5

QUEEN ELIZABETH II'S SILVER JUBILEE, 1977

The Queen's silver jubilee brought about major celebrations around the Commonwealth throughout 1977. These celebrations coincided with a Royal Tour of Her Majesty's various Realms that took her and The Duke of Edinburgh to Fiji, Tonga, Australia, New Zealand, Papua New Guinea, and the Caribbean, concluding their travels in Canada. The Royal Couple, accompanied by The Prince of Wales, touched down in Ottawa on 14 October for a five-day tour packed with more than 30 events and engagements.

One of the highlights of the silver jubilee tour occurred on 18 October when The Queen and The Duke of Edinburgh attended Parliament. Her Majesty read the Speech from the Throne in the Senate Chamber, which was packed with federal politicians, officials, and invited guests: "Whenever I am in this wonderful country of Canada, with her vast resources and unlimited challenges, I feel thankful that Canadians have been so successful in establishing a vigorous democracy well suited to a proud and free people."[1] The Queen proceeded to deliver the most extensive address of her reign in Canada, as she outlined the legislative program for the session ahead as set out by Prime Minister Pierre Trudeau.

Queen Elizabeth II, accompanied by The Duke of Edinburgh, reads the Speech from the Throne during the Silver Jubilee Tour of Canada, 1977.

In addition to celebrations in Ottawa, events were held in provincial and territorial capitals across Canada and at the local level by many different service organizations. Aside from the 1977 Royal Tour, the Silver Jubilee Medal program formed the central element of the overall commemorative activities. The Commemorative Medal for the Silver Jubilee of Her Majesty Queen Elizabeth II followed the tradition set when a special medal was struck for King George V's silver jubilee in 1935. The British government announced the creation of a Silver Jubilee Medal on 15 November 1976, and this led to calls for a similar program in Canada. Unlike Australia and New Zealand, which both decided to utilize the issue of Silver Jubilee Medal that was designed for the United Kingdom, the Canadian government decided to develop a different design for the reverse of the Canadian issue. The overall purpose and criteria used for the bestowal of the Silver Jubilee Medal throughout the Commonwealth was similar. The Canadian program was officially launched on 6 February 1977, with Her Majesty approving the Canadian design on 18 May 1977. The distribution of the medal was administered by the Department of the Secretary of State in cooperation with the Office of the Secretary to the Governor General.

Celebrations were held across the country throughout the year with events culminating in the 1977 Royal Tour. The Silver Jubilee Medal was awarded to Canadian citizens who were deemed to have made a significant contribution to their community, province, or the country as a whole. Recipients were selected by a variety of government officials, non-governmental organizations, and politicians. All living members of the Order of Canada and the Order of Military Merit were automatically awarded the medal, along with the living recipients of the Victoria Cross, the George Cross, and the Cross of Valour.

For the military the distribution to members of Her Majesty's Canadian Forces was quite rigid and resulted in dissatisfaction among many members of the CF. Distribution of the medal was in part based on rank, and awards were not spread evenly across all ranks of the CF on the basis of proportion. For example, all flag and general officers were awarded the medal, while 50 percent of colonels, 25 percent of lieutenant-colonels, 20 percent of majors, and 5 percent of captains and lieutenants were recipients. This left 4,000 medals for the remaining ranks, with the distribution similarly broken down to 50 percent of chief warrant officers, 25 percent of master warrant officers, 15 percent of warrant officers, and 5 percent of sergeants and master corporals receiving the medal. While merit and length of service were the primary considerations, the favourable allocation of medals to those in senior positions resulted in a number of negative articles in the press.

Queen Elizabeth II's Silver Jubilee Medal obverse.

Queen Elizabeth II's Silver Jubilee Medal reverse.

The silver jubilee marked the first time that Canada did not use the Commonwealth issue of the coronation/jubilee medal and that a unique Canadian design was commissioned. While the overall design of the medal and its ribbon were shared with the Commonwealth issue, the reverse of the medal remained specific to Canada.

An early design executed by Bruce Beatty, CM, CD, included two sprigs of 24 maples leaves (two for each province and territory), along with the Royal Cypher. However, this was deemed to be too traditional in appearance, and a small competition was held among four artists. From their designs the silver jubilee committee of the Department of the Secretary of State selected two options. The first depicted a sprig of two

Plaster rendering of the Silver Jubilee Medal reverse.

maple leaves in their natural form, with the text 25 YEARS/ANS CANADA in the foreground. While the Committee unanimously approved of this design, when it was presented to the secretary of state, he vetoed the decision and went with the single maple leaf design that ended up appearing on the medal. The secretary of state was concerned that the two maple leaves might be construed as representing English and French as separate elements of Canadian society. The chair of the committee, Graham Glockling, LVO, noted in a memo to the design committee that "the Secretary of State, the Honourable John Roberts, has selected the second design submitted by Mrs. Hunt."[2] At this point there was still no Royal Cypher on the

Draft design for the Silver Jubilee reverse by Bruce Beatty.

medal or anything on the reverse to directly link the medal to The Queen. The Royal Cypher was added at the bottom of the medal at the direction of Esmond Butler, the secretary to the governor general.

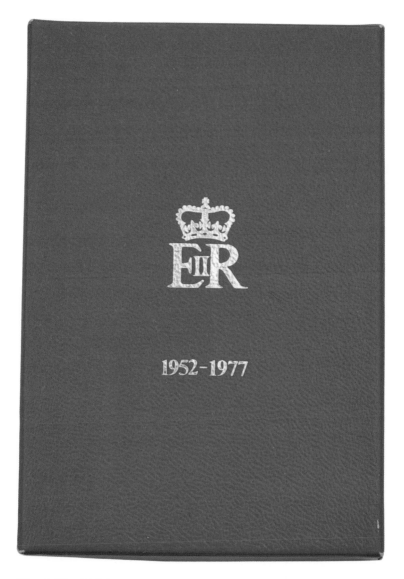

Silver Jubilee Medal transmittal box (gentleman's version).

The silver medal is 32 mm in diameter. The obverse bears a crowned effigy of The Queen circumscribed by the words ELIZABETH II DEI GRATIA REGINA FID. DEF. The reverse bears a stylized maple leaf with the word CANADA above and the dates *1952–1977* below, separated by the Royal Cypher. The medal was struck from sterling silver by the Royal Canadian Mint. While the obverse was designed by David Wynn on behalf of the Royal Mint in London, the reverse was designed by Canadian artist Dora de Pédery-Hunt, OC, OOnt.

The Silver Jubilee Medal is hung from a claw-footed suspender with a small hollow ball on top through which a silver ring passes. The ribbon is 32 mm watered white, with a 2 mm blue stripe lining either edge and a central 2 mm red stripe bordered on either side by 3 mm of blue.

The medal was presented in a small red cardboard transmittal box with a flip lid impressed with the Royal Cypher in silver, along with the dates *1952–1977*. A grey-brown-coloured certificate was issued with each medal. The 1977 jubilee logo was embossed in

Queen Elizabeth II's Silver Jubilee Medal certificate.

silver at the top of the certificate, and the name of the recipient was computer-printed in the middle. The signature of Governor General Jules Léger was printed in the upper-right-hand corner. In all 10 special certificates were issued with names inscribed in calligraphy. These were presented to the governor general, his consort, the prime minister, former governors general and their spouses, and a number of other senior state officials. The award was generally issued unnamed, although those personally presented by Governor General Léger and those awarded to Government House staff members were officially impressed in block capitals with the person's full name (e.g., JOYCE BRYANT).

The first investiture took place late on the afternoon of 31 October in the long gallery at Rideau Hall where Governor General Léger invested 33 members of the viceregal household with the medal.

Silver Jubilee Medal transmittal box (lady's version).

DISTRIBUTION OF THE COMMEMORATIVE MEDAL FOR THE SILVER JUBILEE OF HER MAJESTY QUEEN ELIZABETH II

Group	Number	Total
Those in the Table of Precedence	1 each	1,225
Governor General's List		100
Lieutenant Governors' Lists	10 each	100
Prime Minister's Staff		15
Cabinet Ministers' Lists		300
Senior Civil Servants		240
Holders of VC, GC, and CV	1 each	50
Order of Canada	1 each	1,000
Order of Military Merit	1 each	600
Northwest Territories and Yukon Territory		62
National Organizations		7,100
Special Groups		102
Public Service of Canada		2,700
Provincial Public Services		2,700
Education		1,000
Native Peoples		300
Municipal Officials (allocated depending on population)		1,796
Canadian Forces		7,000
Police		1,000
Firemen		300
Royal Canadian Mounted Police		650
Veterans' Organizations		1,000
Reserve (extra medals for special issue and for use as replacements)		560
TOTAL		**30,000**

The Commonwealth issue of the Silver Jubilee Medal saw 6,870 medals bestowed upon Australians, 1,507 on New Zealanders, and 30,000 upon people in the United Kingdom, with 9,000 awarded to the British Armed Forces and the balance to civilians. The medal criteria in Australia, New Zealand, and the United Kingdom were similar to that used for the Canadian program, and medals were given to members of the respective armed forces as well as to civilians.

The Commonwealth issue of the Silver Jubilee Medal was also 32 mm in diameter, struck in sterling silver by the Royal Mint in London. The obverse of the Canadian and Commonwealth issues was identical, while the reverse of the Commonwealth issue bore the inscription THE 25TH YEAR OF THE REIGN OF QUEEN ELIZABETH II 6TH FEBRUARY 1977, circumscribed with a wreath of silver-birch foliage and catkins. Silver jubilee celebrations in Britain included a tour of Scotland, a service of thanksgiving held at St. Paul's Cathedral on 7 June, and a Royal Review of the Fleet at Spithead on 28 June where Her Majesty reviewed 175 ships. The Silver Jubilee year concluded with a visit to Hong Kong followed by a Commonwealth-wide address by The Queen on Christmas Day.

Queen Elizabeth II's Silver Jubilee
Medal (Commonwealth Realms
issue) reverse.

6

125TH ANNIVERSARY OF CONFEDERATION, 1992

The enduring success achieved with the centennial celebrations held across Canada in 1967 played no small part in the desire to re-create the same national enthusiasm as the country approached the 125th anniversary of Confederation. As in 1967, there were practical political considerations that helped to push the Canada 125 program into being. Notably, these included ongoing tensions surrounding national unity and a desire to improve federal-provincial relations by giving all citizens a greater feeling of pride in their country, regardless of where they lived.

Despite the patriation of the Constitution in 1982, the marathon of constitutional negotiations that commenced with Prime Minister Pearson in the late 1960s was far from over. The Province of Quebec had never signed onto the new constitution, and this unsatisfactory situation was one that then Prime Minister Brian Mulroney wanted to rectify. In 1987 this resulted in the drafting of the Meech Lake Accord, which would have seen Quebec become a signatory of the 1982 Constitution in return for recognition of the province as a distinct society, while increasing provincial power in a number of areas. It also included a change to the constitutional amending formula. The accord ultimately failed due to opposition from Manitoba and Newfoundland. Out of this came the creation of the Citizen's Forum on National Unity, which was established by the federal government to determine what constitutional changes Canadians wanted. From this flowed the Charlottetown Accord, which was negotiated between the federal and provincial governments in 1991–92, and subsequently defeated by a national referendum in October 1992.

The endless constitutional negotiations caused tension between Ottawa and many of the provinces. There was a strong desire to promote national unity and pride in Canada, despite the ongoing constitutional rancor, and Canada's 125th anniversary was seen as one means of achieving this in a manner similar to the centennial celebrations.

The Canada 125 celebrations also coincided with the 40th anniversary of The Queen's accession to the throne, and many official events across Canada incorporated this milestone into the broader Confederation celebrations. Her Majesty came for a short three-day tour, arriving in Ottawa on 30 June and departing the day after Canada Day.

The Queen presided over national celebrations on Parliament Hill in the presence of more than 65,000 spectators. This was followed by an official dinner hosted by the prime minister and Her Majesty's Canadian Government at the Museum of Civilization in Gatineau. Despite the brevity of the trip, The Queen participated in more than a dozen events, including a luncheon marking the 25th anniversary of her establishment of the Order of Canada and the unveiling of stained glass windows at Rideau Hall, along with a number of plaques. At the provincial level, in most provinces, lieutenant governors and premiers participated in celebratory events similar to those held in Ottawa, all with the assistance of funding from the Canada 125 program, which was administered by the Department of the Secretary of State — the forerunner of the Department of Canadian Heritage. One of the lasting legacies of the Canada 125 celebrations was the creation of the Trans-Canada Trail, a winding recreational path that traverses the country.

Overall, the Canada 125 program supported a diverse array of community, province-wide, and national celebrations and funded everything from bumper stickers, lapel pins, and flags to instructions on how to hold a Canada Day party in your locality.

The Commemorative Medal for the 125th Anniversary of Confederation of Canada, or Canada 125 Medal, was created as part of the Canada 125 celebration program, with the medal being formally established on 7 May 1992.

125th Anniversary of Confederation Commemorative Medal obverse.

125th Anniversary of Confederation Commemorative Medal reverse.

The medal was awarded to people who made a significant contribution to the well-being of their fellow citizens, their community, or to Canada. Recipients were selected by a variety of government officials, non-governmental national organizations, and elected and appointed politicians. It was originally intended that 50,000 medals would be awarded. However, only 42,000 were issued due to problems with the program's administration and a lack of nominations. The experience of the Canada 125 Medal program was to pave the way for the success met by the Golden Jubilee Medal program in 2002, and allow for the involvement of a wide range of NGOs and provincial partners in future commemorative medal programs.

Created by Bruce Beatty, CM, CD, the design of the Canada 125 Medal was a slightly updated version of the Centennial Medal. Blue replaced the red for the edges of the ribbon, representing the Atlantic and Pacific Oceans that border Canada and linking with Canada's motto "from sea to sea," which also appears, in Latin, on the reverse of the medal. To reduce costs, the straight bar

125th Anniversary of Confederation Commemorative Medal certificate.

Canada 125 Medal transmittal box.

suspension was simplified so that the medal was struck in one piece and the medal was not struck in sterling silver as had been the case with all commemorative medals issued to Canadians since 1911.

The insignia is a circular, silver-coloured medal, 36 mm in diameter. The obverse bears the Royal Cypher, superimposed on a natural maple leaf, circumscribed by the words CONFEDERA-TION — CONFÉDÉRATION, with the dates *1867–1992* in the base. The reverse bears the shield of the Royal Arms of Canada, encir-

cled by the motto of the Order of Canada and surmounted by the crest of Canada, with the national motto A MARI USQUE AD MARE at the bottom. The medal is made of a copper and zinc alloy, rhodium-plated, issued unnamed, and was manufactured by two private firms; Rideau Ltée and Guthrie Woods Ltd. The medal is attached to a straight suspender that has a maple leaf in the centre. Through this passes a 32 mm wide ribbon, white in colour, edged on either side by a 4.5 mm stripe of blue, with five 1 mm red stripes, each repre-senting a quarter-century since Confederation (the Centennial Medal has four such stripes) equally spaced between the two blue stripes. An alternate design reversed

Alternate Canada 125 Medal ribbon design.

the proportions of the red and white element of the ribbon. However, this option was discarded as it too closely resembled the ribbon of the Canadian Forces' Decoration.

The Canada 125 Medal was issued in a blue cardboard transmittal box with the Royal Arms of Canada and the dates *1867– 1992* stamped in silver on the lid. Medals were awarded with a certificate printed on heavy white paper. The Royal Arms of Canada were impressed in silver at the top with the signature of

Approved design for the Canada 125 Medal signed by The Queen.

Governor General Ray Hnatyshyn. The name of each recipient was printed on the certificate along with the facsimile signature of the governor general.

DISTRIBUTION OF THE COMMEMORATIVE MEDAL FOR THE 125TH ANNIVERSARY OF CONFEDERATION

Group	Number	Total
Those in the Table of Precedence	1 each	1,500
Governor General's List		170
Lieutenant Governors' Lists	17 each	204
Prime Minister's List		170
Cabinet Ministers' Lists	57 each	2,166
Senators' Lists	40 each	4,160
MPs' Lists	40 each	10,240
Holders of VC, GC, and CV	1 each	18
Members of the Order of Canada	1 each	2,500
Province and Territories (by population)		10,916
National Organizations		7,000
Special Groups		356
Public Service of Canada		5,000
Canadian Forces		4,000
Royal Canadian Mounted Police		1,000
Reserve (extra medals for special issue and for use as replacements)		600
TOTAL		**50,000**

7

QUEEN ELIZABETH II's GOLDEN JUBILEE, 2002

The Queen's golden jubilee marked only the second time in Canada's post-Confederation history that a monarch had observed half a century on the throne. The federal government mounted an extensive program of celebrations across the country along with significant provincial and territorial involvement. Her Majesty The Queen and His Royal Highness The Duke of Edinburgh began their 12-day visit on 4 October, landing in the newly established territory of Nunavut, where she addressed the Territorial Legislature and attended a number of cultural events. This was followed by tours of Victoria and Vancouver in British Columbia where The Queen famously dropped the puck at a National Hockey League game between the Vancouver Canucks and the San Jose Sharks. The Royal Couple then headed on to Winnipeg for the rededication of the Golden Boy statue that sits atop the Manitoba Legislature and for an outing on the Red River.

In Hamilton, Ontario, as Colonel-in-Chief, The Queen presented new regimental colours to the Argyle and Sutherland Highlanders in Copps Coliseum. A variety of events were later held in Toronto where Her Majesty celebrated the 50th anniversary of the Canadian Broadcasting Corporation at CBC Centre. It was then on to New Brunswick where The Queen had last visited in 1984. The Royal Couple toured the newly reopened Old Government House and met with the inaugural members of the recently established Order of New Brunswick. This was followed by a performance of the New Brunswick Youth Orchestra. His Royal Highness attended a reception for the 2nd Battalion of the Royal Canadian Regiment, of which

Her Majesty The Queen dropping the puck at General Motors Place, Vancouver, 6 October 2002.

he is Colonel-in-Chief. In addition, the Royal Couple attended events held at Sussex Elementary School and opened a new wing of the school while interacting with many young citizens.

After their tour of eastern Canada, the Royal Couple journeyed to Ottawa for the obligatory visit to the nation's capital for an official dinner hosted by Her Majesty's Canadian Government, along with a luncheon hosted at Rideau Hall in honour of the 35th anniversary of The Queen's establishment of the Order of Canada. The visit concluded on 15 October, and the Royal Couple departed Ottawa Airport for London, England.

While the 2002 Royal Visit had been meticulously planned in advance of the jubilee, there was a lack of enthusiasm among senior federal officials and politicians to embark upon a commemorative medal program. The memory of the controversy experienced with the 125th Anniversary of Confederation Medal was still fresh in the minds of some, and there was muted concern about how members of the Bloc Québécois would receive the program. As it turned out, the governor general, the prime minister, and the minister of Canadian Heritage were

Her Majesty The Queen in New Brunswick, 11 October 2002.

inundated with correspondence calling for the establishment of a Golden Jubilee Medal, and despite significant bureaucratic opposition, a program was hastily established at the insistence of Prime Minister Jean Chrétien. Her Majesty The Queen assented to the creation of the medal on 23 February 2002. On 12 March the governor general issued a press release announcing the establishment of the Golden Jubilee Medal program. Commonly known as the Queen's Golden Jubilee Medal, the medal's formal designation is the Commemorative Medal for Her Majesty Queen Elizabeth II's Golden Jubilee.

The total number of recipients was set at 46,000, and in the broadest sense, the program followed the same pattern as that used for previous commemorative medals in Canada, providing a balance of civilian and military recognition. The medal was awarded to Canadian citizens (alive as of 6 February 2002) who had made a significant contribution to Canada or to a particular province, territory, region, or community within Canada, or who had made an outstanding achievement abroad that brought credit to Canada. Recipients were nominated by members of the general public through a number of partners in the program, including the governor general, the prime minister, the lieutenant governors, the territorial commissioners, senators, members of Parliament, the Canadian Forces, the Royal Canadian Mounted Police, federal public service, and provincial governments, as well as 175 non-governmental organizations.

The medal itself is a circular gold-coloured medal, 32 mm in diameter. The obverse bears an effigy of Her Majesty Queen Elizabeth wearing the George IV diadem, circumscribed by the legend REINE DU CANADA — QUEEN OF CANADA. Designed by Dora de Pédery-Hunt, OC, OOnt, this effigy is the one that was used on Canadian coinage from 1990 to 2002. The reverse bears the Royal Crown above a single maple leaf, upon which is superimposed the Royal Cypher, all of which is circumscribed by 1952 — CANADA — 2002. Designed by a committee at the Chancellery of Honours, the medal was struck by the Royal Canadian Mint and made from gold-plated bronze. The suspender is a single loop (eyelet) through which a ring passes for the ribbon. The ribbon was a new permutation of the traditional colours red, white, and blue and was 32 mm in width. The outer stripes of the ribbon are red and 2 mm wide, followed by 10 mm royal blue stripes, followed by 3 mm white stripes and a single 2 mm red stripe down the centre. Designed in the United Kingdom, the same ribbon was used for the British issue.

Each medal was issued in a blue cardboard transmittal box, with the Canadian golden jubilee logo (the Royal Cypher with a

flourish of maple leaves along with the numeral 50) stamped in gold on the lid. Awards came with a white certificate bearing the golden jubilee logo in full

Queen Elizabeth II's Golden Jubilee Medal obverse.

Queen Elizabeth II's Golden Jubilee Medal reverse.

colour at the top and the 50th anniversary of Canadian governors general logo at the bottom, with the recipient's name laser-printed in the centre.

The claw-footed suspender that was included in the original drawing of the Golden Jubilee Medal and authorized by Her Majesty proved to be too problematic for the Royal Canadian Mint to manufacture. When the mint struck the Silver Jubilee Medal in 1977, it had subcontracted the production of the suspender, but in 2002, due to time and budgetary constraints, plans for the claw-footed suspender were abandoned in favour of an eyelet ring suspender.

The Royal Canadian Mint also held the contract for the administration of the program. The mint provided an electronic template to the partners, who completed it and returned it to the mint where the names were entered in the database to verify for duplicates. Then the mint printed the certificate and included it in each individual package, which also included the medal in its

On the occasion of the fiftieth Anniversary of the accession of HER MAJESTY THE QUEEN to the Throne the Golden Jubilee Medal is presented to

À l'occasion du cinquantième anniversaire de l'accession de SA MAJESTÉ LA REINE au Trône la Médaille du jubilé est remise à

Mr. Bruce Patterson, B.A., B.Ed., F.H.S.C.

CANADIAN GOVERNORS GENERAL 1952-2002 LES GOUVERNEURS GÉNÉRAUX CANADIENS

Queen Elizabeth II's Golden Jubilee Medal certificate.

Golden Jubilee Medal transmittal box.

transmittal box, a wearing guide, and a letter providing information on the medal. Medal packages were shipped to the partners for presentation.

The Golden Jubilee Medal also marked another innovation: the publication of the list of recipients in an interactive online database that allowed citizens to look up names. Up to this point, only those appointed to the Order of Canada and the Order of Military Merit and recipients of the three Decorations for Bravery could be searched through an online database.

The Canadian Golden Jubilee Medal program differed significantly from the British Golden Jubilee Medal program that saw 355,000 medals awarded and presented to serving members of the British Armed Forces, Her Majesty's Coast Guard, the Royal National Lifeboat Institution, and police, fire, prison, and ambulance services. The criteria for the British Golden Jubilee Medal required the completion of five or more years of service in any of the aforementioned services as of 6 February 2002. In addition to recognizing members of the protective services, a small number of medals were awarded to members of the Royal Household in the United Kingdom.

The British Golden Jubilee Medal was struck by the Royal Mint in gold-plated cupro-nickel. The obverse depicted a right-facing effigy of Queen Elizabeth II wearing the Royal Crown, while the reverse depicted the shield from the Royal Arms of the United Kingdom surmounted by the St. Edward's Crown, circumscribed by the dates *1952* and *2002*. The British issue employed the same ribbon as its Canadian counterpart and was packaged in a white cardboard transmittal box with the Royal Cypher, the name of the medal, and dates impressed in gold on the lid. Uniquely, the box also contained a certificate of authenticity from the Royal Mint as well as a length of ribbon for court mounting.

The inaugural Golden Jubilee Medal investiture was held in front of Rideau Hall on 29 June 2002 and was presided over by

Governor General Adrienne Clarkson. This event was held in conjunction with the annual viceregal garden party. Eighteen citizens were invested, each chosen to represent their province and community as an example of outstanding citizenship and devotion to service. One recipient represented each of the 10 provinces and three territories, four represented the Canadian Forces (Navy, Army, Air Force, and Reserve), and one represented the RCMP. The first recipients were Paul Birckel, Whitehorse, Yukon; Vernon C. Brink, Vancouver, British Columbia; Petty Officer 2nd Class Marie Gisèle Dianne Chénier,

Ancienne Lorette, Quebec; Mary Deigham, Kinkora, Prince Edward Island; Paul Delage Roberge, Brossard, Quebec; Lyn Goldman, Regina, Saskatchewan; Noel

Queen Elizabeth II's Golden Jubilee Medal (British issue) obverse.

Queen Elizabeth II's Golden Jubilee Medal (British issue) reverse.

Knockwood, Dartmouth, Nova Scotia; the Honourable Justice Graydon Nicholas, Fredericton, New Brunswick; Sierra Noble, Winnipeg, Manitoba; Master Seaman J.B. Oliver, Shearwater, Nova Scotia; Elisapee Ootoova, Pond Inlet, Nunavut; Barbara Poole, Edmonton, Alberta; Corporal R.P. Riddiford, Petawawa, Ontario; Oliver Rose, Bishops Falls, Newfoundland and Labrador; RCMP Constable Leslie Wayne Russett, Ottawa, Ontario; Corporal M. Schlegle, Patricia Bay, British Columbia; and Tommy Wright, Inuvik, Northwest Territories. The last time a formal inaugural investiture was held for a commemorative medal was in 1935 during King George V's silver jubilee.

DISTRIBUTION OF THE COMMEMORATIVE MEDAL FOR THE GOLDEN JUBILEE OF HER MAJESTY QUEEN ELIZABETH II

Group	Number	Total
Those in the Table of Precedence	1 each	1,500
Governor General's List		170
Lieutenant Governors' Lists	20 each	1,000*
Prime Minister's List		170
Cabinet Ministers' Lists	10 each	360†
Senators' Lists	20 each	2,100
MPs' Lists	20 each	6,020
Holders of VC, GC, and CV	1 each	15
Members of the Order of Canada	1 each	2,900
Provinces and Territories (by population)		7,000§
National Organizations/Non-Governmental Organizations		10,000
Special Groups		356
Federal Government		4,000
Canadian Forces		8,000
Royal Canadian Mounted Police		2,200

Reserve (extra medals for special issue and for use as replacements)		1,035
TOTAL		**46,470**

* The allocation for each lieutenant governor and territorial commissioner was based on 20 medals each to which was added a proportion of medals based on the provincial population. Thus the lieutenant governor of Ontario received more than 200 medals to distribute.

† Each minister received 10 medals in addition to an allocation of 20 medals as an MP for a total of 30 medals each.

§ The allocation for each province was based on 100 medals each to which was added a proportion of medals based on the provincial population.

As per tradition, the dignitaries on the Table of Precedence for Canada were automatically awarded the medal. Usually, this was limited to the most senior dignitaries, but for this program the entire table was included, both at the federal and provincial or territorial levels, down to all provincial elected officials and court judges. This added up to over 3,500 medals, much more than the 1,500 estimate based on the numbers from the Canada 125 Medal program. By contrast, in 2012, the awards to the Table of Precedence reverted to the higher end of the federal table only, provincial governments being free to use their own provincial allocation to recognize their dignitaries as they wished. Automatic awards also included, by custom, holders of the highest decorations and all members of the Order of Canada.

As the program evolved, some partners decided not to participate or did not use their full allocation. Unused medals were thus reallocated to interested partners. As an example, while the Canadian Forces were initially allocated 8,000 medals, they were granted many unused medals at the end of the program and eventually awarded 9,660 medals to their members. It should be noted that the Canadian Forces used a computer-generated selection based on length of service in each rank in each trade and each service of the Canadian Forces. This selection process was controversial within the CF given that it did not take merit into account. It was therefore not repeated in 2012.

As expected, participation in Quebec was problematic. Not surprisingly, the Parti Québécois provincial government refused to participate, and the leader of the Bloc Québécois in the House of Commons directed his MPs not to participate. Nineteen Bloquistes complied with the order, while 16 Bloc MPs did award medals, some of them even asking for more. The leader of the Bloc Québécois eventually relented and awarded a few medals himself to veterans in his riding.

The Queen's Golden Jubilee Medal program was well received by the public, and despite some minor problems, was deemed a great success and a model to be emulated for future commemorative medal programs.

8

The Provincial Centennials — Saskatchewan and Alberta, 2005

T he inclusion of provincial honours in the national order of precedence for wearing orders, decorations, and medals, and recognition of them as provincial honours of the Crown, is a relatively recent development. What began with the incorporation of the provincial orders of merit into the national order of precedence has now extended to commemorative medals.

Since the establishment of the Canadian honours system in 1967, there had been a number of attempts by various provinces to have provincial commemorative medals approved for wear with national honours. One notable case occurred in advance of the bicentennial of the establishment of Upper Canada in 1984 when the Government of Ontario struck the Ontario Bicentennial Medal. At the time the Government of Canada refused to give the award any official recognition, despite it being styled like other commemorative medals — a disc and suspender hung from a 32 mm multicoloured rainbow ribbon.

Her Majesty The Queen presenting a stone plaque to First Nations University of Canada.

In 2005 Her Majesty The Queen and His Royal Highness The Duke of Edinburgh made an eight-day tour of Saskatchewan and Alberta as part of the centennial celebrations marking each province's entry into Confederation. From 17 to 25 of May the Royal Couple undertook a variety of events in each province, beginning in Saskatchewan where The Queen visited First Nations University of Canada where she unveiled a plaque and met with Prime Minister Paul Martin. The following day Her Majesty unveiled a bronze equestrian statute of herself at the provincial legislature during a torrential downpour. Then it was off to Lumsden in the Qu'Appelle Valley. At the RCMP Depot Division in Regina the Royal Couple paid their respect to the memory of four Mounties who had recently fallen in the line of duty. In Saskatoon they went on a walking tour of Canadian Light Source, a synchrotron, the day being capped off with a cultural performance at Saskatoon Credit Union Centre before tens of thousands of citizens.

Upon arriving in Alberta, The Queen was welcomed by 25,000 at Commonwealth Stadium in Edmonton and then proceeded to unveil a plaque giving Royal designation to the Royal Alberta Museum. This was followed by The Duke of Edinburgh making a tour of the oil sands in Fort McMurray and meeting local First Nations and Métis representatives. Later, during the tour Her Majesty addressed the Alberta Legislature and unveiled new stained glass windows in the building. In Calgary the Government of Alberta held an official luncheon followed by a centennial free public concert held in Pengrowth Saddledome, featuring Alberta's multicultural heritage. On 25 May the Royal Couple departed Canada, returning only five years later in Halifax on 28 June 2010.

The idea behind the Commemorative Medal for the Centennial of Saskatchewan, commonly known as the Saskatchewan Centennial Medal, came from the province's then chief of protocol, Dr. D. Michael Jackson, CVO, SOM, CD. Planning for the Saskatchewan Centennial Medal program began nearly three years before the actual events. Jackson had been involved with both the Canada 125 Medal and Golden Jubilee Medal programs and felt that a province-specific commemorative medal would be an appropriate way to help mark Saskatchewan's centennial of entering Canadian Confederation as a province.

The medal was established by an amendment to the *Provincial Emblems and Honours Act*, which was granted Royal Assent by Lieutenant Governor Lynda Haverstock on 27 May 2003.

As with other commemorative medals, the criteria included a broad range of contributions to the community and to the province through leadership, voluntarism, community involvement, and outstanding personal achievements. Recipients were nominated by federal members of Parliament from Saskatchewan, members of the Provincial Legislative Assembly, a number of

volunteer organizations, and the lieutenant governor. The inaugural investiture took place on 1 January 2005 at the Saskatchewan Legislative Building, where 13 recipients

Saskatchewan Centennial Medal obverse.

Saskatchewan Centennial Medal reverse.

were invested by Haverstock. The final investiture took place on 31 May 2006, by which point 4,200 medals had been awarded.

The medal is a circular bronze medal, 36 mm in diameter. The obverse depicts a Royal Crown in the centre atop three prairie lilies with the provincial motto on a scroll below, the whole circumscribed by the text SASKATCHEWAN 1905–2005. The reverse bears the provincial shield on a plain matte finished field. Hung from a straight suspender, the 32 mm wide ribbon is gold in colour with a 2 mm green stripe inset 2 mm from each edge of the ribbon. The medal was designed by Warwick Communications of Saskatoon and was struck by Bond Boyd Ltd. of Toronto. Non-residents of Saskatchewan were also eligible to receive the medal, although fewer than 50 were awarded to non-residents.

The Saskatchewan Centennial Medal was awarded with a certificate signed by Lieutenant Governor Lynda Haverstock as well as by Premier Lorne Calvert. The medal was issued in a green rectangular transmittal box with gold stampings on the lid.

Saskatchewan Centennial Medal certificate.

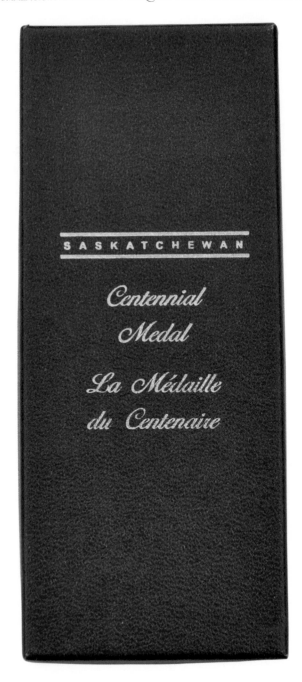

Saskatchewan Centennial Medal transmittal box.

Alberta followed the path set by Saskatchewan and established the Alberta Centennial Medal with the *Alberta Centennial Medal Act*, which was granted Royal Assent by the lieutenant governor of Alberta on 24 March 2005.

The medal was awarded to recognize those who had made a significant contribution to their fellow citizens, to their community, and to Alberta. Recipients were nominated by federal members of Parliament from Alberta, members of the Provincial Legislative Assembly, 200 volunteer organizations, and the lieutenant governor. Nearly 8,000 medals were presented. When the medal was established, it was only open to residents of the province, although this was changed to allow non-residents to receive the honour. Fewer than 100 medals were presented to non-residents.

A gold-plated bronze medal, 36 mm in diameter, the obverse bears the full provincial coat of arms and is circumscribed by the text ALBERTA CENTENNIAL 1905–2005. The reverse bears a large Canadian maple leaf with the provincial shield in the centre, circumscribed with the text HONOURING OUTSTANDING ALBERTANS. The medal was designed by John Smith of Artsmith Communications in Edmonton. The suspender, a ring attached to the disc of the medal through which another smaller ring passes and attaches the disc to a straight suspender bar, remains unique among Canadian commemorative medals. It was modelled on the suspender used for the Canadian Volunteer Service Medal, which was issued following the Second World War.

Alberta Centennial Medal obverse.

The ribbon of the Alberta Centennial Medal is 32 mm wide edged on each side with 3 mm of blue, 3 mm of gold, 2 mm of green, 2 mm of white, and a central 1 mm stripe of pink. The blue represents clear skies and sparkling lakes; gold — wheat fields and resource wealth; green — forests; white — mountains; pink — the wild rose, which is the provincial flower. The medal was presented in a rectangular blue cardboard transmittal box with gold stampings and was issued with a certificate signed by Lieutenant Governor Norman Kwong and Premier Ralph Klein.

As we approach 2017 and the sesquicentennial of Confederation, it is conceivable that the four founding provinces of Canada — Ontario, Quebec, Nova Scotia, and New Brunswick — will attempt to establish medal programs along the lines of those executed by Saskatchewan and Alberta in 2005. Indeed, the following years could bring about other sesquicentennial medals for Manitoba (1870–2020), British Columbia (1871–2021), and Prince Edward Island (1873–2023), each marking 150 years in Confederation in the coming decade.

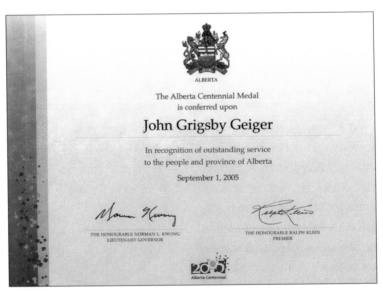

Alberta Centennial Medal certificate.

9

QUEEN ELIZABETH II's DIAMOND JUBILEE, 2012

For only the second time in Canadian history, a diamond jubilee of a reigning Sovereign's accession to the throne is being celebrated. The last such occasion took place in 1897 when Queen Victoria marked 60 years on the throne. During the 2010 Royal Tour of Her Majesty The Queen and His Royal Highness The Duke of Edinburgh, a number of diamond jubilee celebration projects were initiated, notably The Queen's unveiling of the design for the diamond jubilee stained glass window that was subsequently installed above the entrance to the Senate at Parliament in Ottawa. The marquee event for the diamond jubilee year will be a Royal Tour undertaken by Their Royal Highnesses The Prince of Wales and The Duchess of Cornwall. At the national, provincial, and local levels, events have been planned across the country. A central element of the diamond jubilee celebrations is the Diamond Jubilee Medal program, modelled on the highly successful Golden Jubilee Medal program.

On 3 February 2010 the Government of Canada announced that Her Majesty The Queen had approved the design of a medal in honour of the impending diamond jubilee of Her Majesty's accession to the throne.

Queen Elizabeth II's Diamond Jubilee Medal obverse.

Queen Elizabeth II's Diamond Jubilee Medal reverse.

Struck in nickel silver with a claw-footed suspender, the 32 mm medal is silver in colour and displays on the obverse a crowned effigy of The Queen circumscribed by her Canadian titles, ELIZABETH II DEI GRATIA REGINA — CANADA. The reverse bears a diamond with the Royal Cypher in the centre. Protruding from each side of the diamond is a stylized maple leaf, the field being made up of many small diamonds. The dates *1952* and *2012* also appear on the reverse, along with the Latin motto VIVAT REGINA, which translates as "Long Live The Queen."

The medal program was overseen by a subcommittee of the national Diamond Jubilee Committee chaired by the Canadian secretary to The Queen, Kevin S. MacLeod, CVO, CD, and counted among its members Emmanuelle Sajous (deputy secretary, Chancellery), Gabrielle Lappa (director of honours, Chancellery), Denis Poirier (assistant director — Decorations and Medals, Chancellery), Sylvie Barsalou (program manager, Diamond Jubilee Medal, Chancellery), Paul Turcotte (Canadian Heritage), Major Carl Gauthier, MMM, CD (National Defence), Superintendent Greg J. Peters (RCMP), and Peter Mills (Veterans' Affairs).

The medal itself was designed by Fraser Herald Cathy Bursey-Sabourin of the Canadian Heraldic Authority. The ribbon of the medal is yet another permutation of the 1953 Coronation Medal ribbon: a dark red ribbon 32 mm in width is edged with 2 mm of blue, while a 2 mm central stripe of dark red is bordered on each side by a 3 mm stripe of white.

Major Carl Gauthier devised this new version of the ribbon based on the logic used for previous ribbons. When he met with British officials at the Ministry of Defence in Whitehall in 2010, Gauthier discovered they had come up with a different design. After he explained the logic behind the Canadian ribbon design, the British asked if Canada would mind if they used the same variation, thus preserving the tradition of our two countries sharing the same ribbon design for royal commemorative medals. Working together on this issue has also resulted in the restoration of the shades of red and blue used for the 1953 Coronation Medal in this new ribbon. The two colours had become much brighter for the 1977 and 2002 jubilee medals.

The Diamond Jubilee Medal was struck in nickel-silver by the Royal Canadian Mint in Ottawa. The medals are also lacquered to prevent tarnishing. A total of 60,000 medals will be produced, with 11,000 going to members of Her Majesty's Canadian Forces (approximately 10 percent of the total strength of the forces) and 2,300 to members of the Royal Canadian Mounted Police. The balance will be distributed among other protective services, the public service, civilian groups, senior state officials, and volunteers across Canada. This time a reduced portion of the Table of Precedence for Canada was awarded the medal along with all living members of the Order of Canada, holders of the Cross of Valour, and the sole living Canadian recipient of the George Cross, Colonel Arthur Richard Cecil Butson, GC, OMM, CD.

Queen Elizabeth II's Diamond Jubilee Medal certificate.

Diamond Jubilee Medal transmittal box.

While past programs strictly limited eligibility to Canadian citizens, this program included permanent residents and, more interestingly, allowed non-Canadians to receive the medal if they were eligible under the Table of Precedence or the Order of Canada categories. This means that for the first time honorary members of the Order were recognized as well as His Royal Highness The Duke of Edinburgh, who has served as a Canadian Privy Councillor since 1957. The Duke will therefore receive both the British and the Canadian medals.

The transmittal box for the medal is an updated version of the 2002 box, this time in deep red (matching the ribbon), with the jubilee emblem impressed in silver on the lid and a black felt insert to hold the medal.

Painting of Queen Elizabeth II's Diamond Jubilee Medal.

As with the Silver Jubilee Medal certificate, the Canada 125 Medal certificate, and the Golden Jubilee Medal certificate, the governor general's signature appears on the document. The Diamond Jubilee Medal certificate is unique in that the governor general personally signed all 60,000 certificates, having started the process many months before the Diamond Jubilee Medal program formally commenced.

The Royal Canadian Mint, as in 2002, not only manufactured the medal but also managed the administration of the program. The process was fairly similar to that used for the Golden Jubilee Medal with some improvements brought about by modern technology. The main example of this was the fact that the partners could submit their nominations through an online interactive portal. Each partner had its own personalized access and was able to not only submit names and manage its allocation but also verify the status of applications submitted.

The first medal was officially struck by Governor General David Johnston on 6 December 2011 at the Royal Canadian

Governor General David Johnston and Prime Minister Stephen Harper unveiling the design of Queen Elizabeth II's Diamond Jubilee Medal.

Mint's Ottawa plant. On this occasion the governor general noted: "The idea of service is embedded in the reign of Her Majesty."[1] The inaugural investiture was held in the Ballroom at Rideau Hall on 6 February 2012. The governor general invested 60 Canadians with the Diamond Jubilee Medal, a cross-section of Canadian society and geography. While commemorative medals are usually issued unnamed, that is without the recipient's details engraved on the edge, the medals to those first 60 recipients and some senior dignitaries on the Canadian Table of Precedence were all specially engraved with the date of the event on the edge, *2012–II–06*. Later that same day the governor general presided over two more Jubilee Medal investitures, presenting medals to the members of the Canadian Ministry and then later to many state dignitaries such as former governors general, former prime ministers, the chief justice of Canada, the speakers of both houses of Parliament, the chief of the Defence Staff, and the commissioner of the RCMP, among others.

Governor General David Johnston striking the first Diamond Jubilee Medal, Minister of Canadian Heritage James Moore in the background.

Governor General David Johnston and Chair of the Board of Directors of the Mint James B. Love following the striking of the first Diamond Jubilee Medal.

Governor General David Johnston and Prime Minister Stephen Harper, along with the first 60 recipients of Queen Elizabeth II's Diamond Jubilee Medal, Rideau Hall, Ottawa, 6 February 2012.

In addition to the Canadian issue of the Diamond Jubilee Medal, two other medals were struck for The Queen's diamond jubilee. Naturally, one for the United Kingdom and the other for The Queen's eight Caribbean realms: Antigua and Barbuda, Bahamas, Barbados, Grenada, Jamaica, Saint Kitts and Nevis, Saint Lucia, and Saint Vincent and the Grenadines. Both the British and the Caribbean Diamond Jubilee Medals were struck by Worcestershire Medal Service Limited in England.

The United Kingdom issue of the Diamond Jubilee Medal was unveiled by Culture Secretary Jeremy Hunt on 28 June 2011. The British Diamond Jubilee Medal program is largely patterned on its 2002 Golden Jubilee Medal program and focuses predominantly on those serving in the uniformed services. The medal will be bestowed

Queen Elizabeth II's Diamond Jubilee Medal (British issue) obverse.

Queen Elizabeth II's Diamond Jubilee Medal (British issue) reverse.

upon all living holders of the Victoria Cross and the George Cross and members of the Royal Household. The vast majority of medals will be awarded to members of the British Armed Forces, emergency services personnel (police, fire, ambulance), police community support officers, operational prison service personnel, Her Majesty's Coast Guard, and front-line Royal National Lifeboat Institution members who have completed five full calendar years of service as of 6 February 2012.

The medal is 32 mm, the same diameter as the Canadian issue, and follows the same size that has been employed for coronation and jubilee medals since King George V's coronation in 1911. The nickel-silver medal with a claw-footed suspender displays The Queen wearing the Girls of Great Britain and

Queen Elizabeth II's Diamond Jubilee Medal and transmittal box (British issue).

Ireland tiara as sculpted by Ian Rank-Brodley, circumscribed by the text ELIZABETH II DEI GRATIA REGINA FID DEF. This is the same effigy that has been used on United Kingdom coinage since 1998–99. The reverse depicts a stylized diamond defaced with the Royal Cypher, the lower portion of the medal circumscribed with the dates *1952–2012*. The medal was designed by Timothy Noad. It is the first British coronation or jubilee medal not to depict the Sovereign wearing the crown. As mentioned above, the ribbon is the same as for the Canadian medal.

Caribbean Realms Diamond Jubilee Medal ribbon.

Queen Elizabeth II's Diamond Jubilee Medal (Caribbean Realms issue) obverse.

Queen Elizabeth II's Diamond Jubilee Medal (Caribbean Realms issue) reverse.

The criteria for bestowal of the Diamond Jubilee Medal of the Caribbean Realms will be set individually by each of the eight Caribbean islands, and medals will be presented by the governor general in each country. The number of medals awarded will likely be small given that the combined population of the participating countries is just over 3.8 million people.

A rhodium-plated 32 mm medal with a claw-footed suspender, the obverse of the Diamond Jubilee Medal of the Caribbean Realms bears the same effigy of The Queen used for the United Kingdom issue and is circumscribed by the text THE DIAMOND JUBILEE QUEEN ELIZABETH II. The reverse bears the Royal Cypher in the centre, with the text CARIBBEAN REALMS and the dates *1952–2012*. The ribbon is the same as that for the Canadian and United Kingdom medals, with the exception that the 2 mm central stripe is black.

DISTRIBUTION OF QUEEN ELIZABETH II'S DIAMOND JUBILEE MEDAL

Group	Number	Total
Those in the Table of Precedence	1 each	750
Governor General's List		200
Lieutenant Governors' Lists	20 each†	1,000
Prime Minister's List		200
Cabinet Ministers' Lists	50 each	1,900
Senators' Lists	30 each	8,100
MPs' Lists	30 each	3,120
Canadian Secretary to The Queen		25
Holders of the GC and CV	1 each	2,700
Members of the Order of Canada	1 each	
Provinces and Territories (by population)	50 each§	6,000
National Organizations/Non-Governmental Organizations		10,000
Protective Services		4,000

Federal Government (Public Service)		4,000
Canadian Forces		11,000
Royal Canadian Mounted Police		2,300
Municipalities		4,000
Reserve (extra medals for special issue and for use as replacements)		705
TOTAL		**60,000**

†The allocation for each lieutenant governor and territorial commissioner was based on 20 medals each to which was added a proportion of medals based on the provincial population.

§The allocation for each province was based on 50 medals each to which was added a proportion of medals based on the provincial population.

Appendix:

Commemorative Medal Details

Formal and Colloquial Designation	Instrument	Numbers
Commemorative Medal for Her Majesty Queen Elizabeth II's Coronation Coronation Medal, 1953		19,000 (CDN) 129,500 (Commonwealth)†
The Canadian Centennial Medal 1967 Centennial Medal, 1967	Instrument from Prime Minister, 30 May 1966 Approved by Her Majesty The Queen, 27 June 1966	29,500*
Commemorative Medal for Her Majesty Queen Elizabeth II's Silver Jubilee Silver Jubilee Medal, 1977	Canada utilized the British issue of the medal as the basis for establishing the Canadian issue of this medal. Approved by the Government of Canada, 18 May 1977	30,000 (CDN) 6,870 (AU) 1,507(NZ) 30,000 (UK)

Commemorative Medal for the 125th Anniversary of the Confederation of Canada Canada 125 Medal	Order-in-Council P.C. 1992-962, 7 May 1992 Letters Patent, 27 May 1992	42,000*
Commemorative Medal for Her Majesty Queen Elizabeth II's Golden Jubilee Golden Jubilee Medal, 2002	Order-in-Council P.C. 2002-195, 15 February 2002 Letters Patent, 23 February 2002	46,470 (CDN) 355,000 (UK)
Queen Elizabeth II's Diamond Jubilee Medal Diamond Jubilee Medal, 2012	Order-in-Council P.C. 2011-1558, 8 December 2011 Letters Patent, 13 January 2012	60,000 (CDN) 400,000 (UK)
Commemorative Medal for the Centennial of Saskatchewan Saskatchewan Centennial Medal, 2005	Act of Provincial Legislature, Royal Assent granted by the Lieutenant Governor, 27 May 2003	4,200*
Alberta Centennial Medal Alberta Centennial Medal, 2005	Act of Provincial Legislature, Royal Assent granted by the Lieutenant Governor, 24 March 2005	8,000*

* Only applicable to Canada
† Includes awards to Canadians

Notes

Abbreviations Used

DND/DHH Department of National Defence/Directorate of History and Heritage

LAC Library and Archives of Canada

OSGG Office of the Secretary to the Governor General

Introduction

1. Nicholas Dirks, *The Hollow Crown: Ethnohistory of an Indian Kingdom* (Cambridge: Cambridge University Press, 1987), 129.

2. Some of the more recent commemorative medals established include the New Zealand Commemorative Medal, awarded in 1990 to mark the 150th anniversary of the signing of the Treaty of Waitangi and the establishment of New Zealand. In 1993 The Queen in Right of New Zealand established the New Zealand Suffrage Centennial Medal, which commemorated 100 years of women having the vote in New Zealand. For Australia's centennial in 2001 the Australia Centenary Medal was established and awarded to 15,838 citizens.

Chapter 1: Commemorative Medals Throughout the Commonwealth

1. Sir Roy Strong, *Coronation: From the 8th to the 21st Century* (London: Harper Perennial, 2005), 341.

2. *Debrett's Dictionary of the Coronation* (London: Dean and Son Ltd./Gale and Polden Ltd., 1902).

3. Howard N. Cole, *Coronation and Royal Commemorative Medals, 1887–1977* (London: J.B. Hayward and Son, 1977), 2.

4. James Risk, et al. *Royal Service Volume II* (London: Third Millennium Publishing, 2001), Chapter 4.

Chapter 3: Queen Elizabeth II's Coronation, 1953

1. DND/DHH, 1953 Coronation Medal Files, H.F.G. Letson to G.C.E. Stein, Undersecretary of State, 29 January 1953.

2. DND/DHH, 1953 Coronation Medal Files, Minutes of a meeting of the Awards Coordination Committee, 20 January 1953.

Chapter 4: Centennial of Confederation, 1967

1. LAC, RG 24, C-380-18, Group Captain E.R. Emond to Air Commodore G.G. Diamond, 18 October 1961.

2. DND/DHH, 1967 Centennial Medal Files, Memo from Brigadier H.A. Phillips to Armed Forces Council, July 1962.

3. LAC, RG 2, Series 5a, Maurice Lamontagne and Paul Hellyer, Memorandum to Cabinet, Centennial Medal, 11 May 1965.

4. Prime Minister's Office, Press Release, 31 May 1967.

5. DND/DHH, 1967 Centennial Medal Files, Memo to Cabinet, 11 April 1967.

6. Christopher McCreery, *The Canadian Forces' Decoration* (Ottawa: National Defence, 2010), 70–72.

CHAPTER 5: QUEEN ELIZABETH II'S SILVER JUBILEE, 1977

1. *Debates of the Senate of Canada*, Speech from the Throne, 18 October 1977.

2. OSGG, Queen Elizabeth II Silver Jubilee Files, Graham Glockling to the Design Committee, 28 March 1977.

CHAPTER 9: QUEEN ELIZABETH II'S DIAMOND JUBILEE, 2012

1. OSGG, Press Release, 6 December 2011.

BIBLIOGRAPHY

PRIMARY SOURCES

Department of National Defence, Directorate of History and Heritage

Office of the Secretary to the Governor General

Library and Archives Canada, Record Group 2

SECONDARY SOURCES

Alexander, E.G.M. *South African Orders, Decorations and Medals*. Cape Town: Human & Rousseau, 1986.

Blatherwick, John F. *Canadian Orders, Decorations and Medals*. Toronto: Unitrade Press, 2003.

Cole, Howard N. *Coronation and Royal Commemorative Medals, 1887–1977*. London: J.B. Hayward & Son, 1977.

Dirks, Nicholas. *The Hollow Crown: Ethnohistory of an Indian Kingdom*. Cambridge: Cambridge University Press, 1987.

Dorling, H. Taprell. *Ribbons and Medals*. London: George Phillip & Son, 1963.

Fearon, Daniel. *Spink's Catalogue of British Commemorative Medals, 1588 to the Present Day*. London: Spink and Son, 1984.

Galloway, Peter. *The Order of the British Empire*. London: Austin and Son, 1996.

Galloway, Peter, David Stanley, and Stanley Martin. *Royal Service Volume I*. London: Victorian Publishing, 1996.

Haxby, James A. *Striking Impressions: The Royal Canadian Mint and Canadian Coinage*. Ottawa, 1986.

Irwin, Ross. *War Medals and Decorations of Canada*. Guelph, ON: Privately Printed, 1971.

Joslin, Edward Charles. *The Standard Catalogue of British Orders, Decorations and Medals*. London: Spink & Son, 1976.

Maton, Michael. *The National Honours and Awards of Australia*. Kenthurst, New South Wales: Kangaroo Press, 1995.

McCreery, Christopher. *The Canadian Forces' Decoration*. Ottawa: Department of National Defence, 2011.

_____. *The Canadian Honours System*. Toronto: Dundurn Press, 2005.

_____. *On Her Majesty's Service: Royal Honours and Recognition in Canada*. Toronto: Dundurn Press, 2008.

_____. *The Order of Canada: Its Origins, History, and Development*. Toronto: University of Toronto Press, 2005.

Nicholson, Harold. *King George the Fifth: His Life and Reign*. London: Constable Press, 1953.

O'Shea, Phillip. *Honours, Titles, Styles and Precedence in New Zealand*. Wellington: Government Printer, 1977.

Pike, Corinna A.W., and Christopher McCreery. *Canadian Symbols of Authority: Maces, Chains, and Rods of Office*. Toronto: Dundurn Press, 2011.

Risk, James, Herny Pownall, David Stanley, John Tamplin, with Stanley Martin. *Royal Service Volume II*. London: Third Millennium Publishing, 2001.

Strong, Sir Roy. *Coronation: From the 8th to the 21st Century*. London: Harper Perennial, 2005.

Thomas, Wendy. *The Register of Canadian Honours*. Toronto: T.H. Best Printing Company, 1991.

ILLUSTRATION CREDITS

Key
AC: Author Collection
Alcock: Rennie Alcock
DND: Department of National Defence
Glockling: Graham Glockling, LVO
Haynes: Ed Haynes
Hodgins: Glen Hodgins
LAC: Library and Archives Canada
McCord: McCord Museum
OSGG: Office of the Secretary to the Governor General
PCH: Department of Canadian Heritage
Ursual: Eugene Ursual Military Antiquarian
Worcestershire: Worcestershire Medal Service Limited

INDEX